MARLENE NOURBESE PHILIP was born in Tobago in the West Indies in 1947. Having taken her first degree in economics at the University of the West Indies, she completed her studies in Ontario, Canada, and was admitted to the Bar in 1975. She was a practising barrister and solicitor until 1982.

Marlene Nourbese Philip has been a writer and poet since 1968 and her first book of poetry, *Thorns*, was published in 1980. This was followed by her second collection of poems, *Salmon Courage*, in 1983. *Harriet's Daughter* is the author's first novel, and in it she adopts a positive approach to problems such as immigration, exile and language faced by young adults in a multi-racial society.

In 1988 she was awarded the Casa de las Américas literary award and the *Tradewinds* journal prize for her poetry and short-story writing.

MARLENE NOURBESE PHILIP

HARRIET'S DAUGHTER

HEINEMANN

Heinemann International
a division of Heinemann Educational Books Ltd
Halley Court, Jordan Hill, Oxford OX2 8EJ

Heinemann Educational Books (Nigeria) Ltd
PMB 5205, Ibadan
Heinemann Educational Books (Kenya) Ltd
Kijabe Street, PO Box 45314, Nairobi
Heinemann Educational Boleswa
PO Box 10103, Village Post Office, Gaborone, Botswana
Heinemann Educational Books Inc.
70 Court Street, Portsmouth, New Hampshire, 03801, USA
Heinemann Educational Books (Caribbean) Ltd
175 Mountain View Avenue, Kingston 6, Jamaica

LONDON EDINBURGH MELBOURNE SYDNEY
AUCKLAND SINGAPORE MADRID
ATHENS HARARE

© Marlene Nourbese Philip 1988
First published by Heinemann International in the
Caribbean Writers Series in 1988
Reprinted 1988

British Library Cataloguing in Publication Data

Philip, Marlene Nourbese
Harriet's daughter.
I. Title
813 [F]   PR9272.9.P5
ISBN 0-435-98924-3
0-435-98925-1 export

Photoset by Wilmaset, Birkenhead, Wirral
Printed in Great Britain by
Richard Clay Ltd, Bungay, Suffolk

For Bruce, Hardie and Hesper,
and all of Harriet's children

1

Our group – three slaves and me, Harriet, as leader – were walking real fast, making good time. We weren't running; we didn't want to call attention to ourselves. Suddenly I heard a noise. I stopped, held up my hand; everyone stopped too. Yes, there it was, the sound of the slave-owners *and* their dogs, and they were coming fast.

I looked around quickly; there was a hedge, a thick one but not too tall. I motioned for the others to follow me. Quickly I wormed my way through the hedge and lay on the ground. The others followed, and not a minute too soon we were all lying on the damp earth, holding our breaths. Not two feet from us the slave-owners and dogs passed, making a whole heap of noise. Just as quickly they were gone. I stood up and dusted off my clothes.

'Hey you! What are you doing? Get out of there!'

A man was shouting at us from his back door. He looked real mean and angry – so did his dog.

'C'mon guys,' I yelled, 'let's beat it.'

This time we went *over* the hedge. Right behind us was this great big German Shepherd dog, slobbering and barking his head off.

'Boy that was close,' I said.

'Oh he just barks a lot,' someone added.

'He looked real mean though.'

'O.K. guys,' I said, 'we're almost there. Let's run for it.'

We sprinted down the road to Freedom, hauled ourselves

through the broken window and fell laughing on the floor. Zulma and her group were already there waiting for us.

'Yippie! we made it!' someone yelled.

Everyone was laughing. We ran around the room; jumped up and down; slapped each other's palms; thumped each other on the back. We had made it to Freedom from slavery and we were ab-so-lute-ly happy.

'Man dat was close,' Zulma said. 'You know one time we hear dem slave-owners and dogs coming, and all of we crawl under dese cars, man we was scared for so, but dey didn't see we. When dey gone, we come out and put foot to "Freedom".'

We all wanted to talk about what happened. We all did, at the same time, at the tops of our voices.

'Hey guys,' I yelled, 'keep it down, the slave-owners may be passing. What's the time somebody?'

'12.45 Mar . . . I mean Harriet.'

We were suddenly all quiet, the other group hadn't made it; they had been caught – we knew it.

'What do we do now?' someone asked.

'Let's have something to eat,' I said. 'Maybe they'll turn up in a while.' Half an hour later no one had come so one by one we left through the window.

That was the first time we played the Underground Railway Game. Some might say that that was when it all began.

No one did, but if anyone had – asked me that is – I would have said that it all began in the playground at my school, Winona, and *before* the Underground Railway Game. Some people might even say that it really began a long time before that, with me and my parents, but since I began with them you can say *everything* began with them. I prefer to say it began that day in the playground. It was a Monday, Monday the sixteenth of January: that was the day I first met her, my friend Zulma. It was morning recess. I hate morning recess in the winter. All I do is stand around the playground and feel cold. That's what I was doing that day, standing around the playground feeling cold and complaining to Ti-cush about the cold. She hated the cold even more than me. We were bored and my jaw was too frozen for me to do more than grunt my agreement to Ti-cush's favourite comment about the world – 'Life sucks.'

Back then life sure sucked for me: life sucked, my parents sucked, especially my father. My brother sucked and my sister sucked, even the Cosby show sucked – I mean everybody on it was so perrrrfect, cute, rich and black. I mean how could *anybody* be so lucky, *and* with parents that understood them and talked and even discussed THE IMPORTANT THINGS OF LIFE? It was all too much, especially living with a sister who fancied she was a clone of Denise Cosby, and bloody, bloody hell, she *was* pretty, prettier than me. Thank God she was fat, well plump, and she wasn't rich; but she (my sister) – was too much, really too much with her make-up and designer jeans, and all that gunk she put in her hair to make her look like Denise Cosby. So I grunted in agreement with Ti-cush; life did suck, it really did, and I had done nothing to deserve this from life, nothing. I was always being told that I was the one with 'the brains in the family', but I would willingly have given that up for what mattered in this world – style and class.

It was Ti-cush who first suggested we go and see what the group of kids over by the swings were up to. *Finally* it looked like something was happening, so we walked over and I pushed my way to the centre. I saw a girl about my age – fourteen years, ten days and some fifteen hours. She was standing at the centre of the group, and although she is now my best, my ab-so-lute friend, I have to say that she did look a bit strange that day. She was wearing these ribbons – if there is anything you can wear to show how much you lack style and class it's ribbons – big, blue, satin ribbons tied in bows on the ends of her braids. Two thick braids. I know it's not cool to want braids that are not fancy, with beads and all that, but right then and there I wished I had braids like that, real thick and long; but she was crying. It wasn't loud, her crying, but you could see that she was, and somehow it was worse because she wasn't making any noise. My lump of a sister, I thought, should take lessons from her;

3

when she cried, I swear you could hear her all the way to Africa or China. That wasn't a nice thought, and I wasn't proud of it – sort of gross really, but if you could imagine someone crying, yet looking proud so that you didn't feel sorry for her, that was how she looked. She held her head up, and pushed her chin out, as if she was trying to stop the tears running down her face. I noticed her left hand, it was curled into a fist; her right hand was wide open and she was pressing it hard against her coat. That was the second funny thing about her – her coat – not funny ha ha, but funny strange; it was real big for her, almost like a grown-up's coat. I really felt sorry for her and thought that she was just as uncool as me – no style, no class. She kept wiping her hand against the coat like she was trying to wipe away something.

'Hey guys, come on,' I said, turning around to face the other kids – I was now standing close to her – 'can't you see she's crying? Leave her alone.' I put my arm around her shoulders and said to her, 'Come on, let's go.' Everyone moved aside for us, and we walked away.

'What's your name?' I said. She was sobbing, but managed to get out a word that sounded something like Thelma.

'Thelma?'

She shook her head, 'No, Zulma.'

'Zulma?' She nodded and wiped her tears with the backs of her hands. I thought it a really strange name, but I didn't think it was the best time to ask her what it meant and where it came from. Before I could say anything else she continued, sobbing between the words: 'and . . . me . . . a hate . . . it . . . here. Me wish me was . . . back home . . . wit Gran . . . it so cold.'

'Where's home?' I didn't give her a chance to answer. I saw she was shivering, 'Come on, you've got to keep moving, or you'll freeze. Your blood hasn't thickened yet, that's what my mum says about people who have just come here from the West Indies.'

'TTTo . . . TT . . . TTobb . . . ' She couldn't get out the word. She shook her head like she was trying to clear it, then

4

she took a deep breath and slowly, very slowly and very carefully, I still remember it, she said the word, stopping between each syllable: 'To-ba-go.' I knew exactly what she meant, the same thing I mean when I say the word ab-so-lute in that way. It means something extra special, even a little different. I had stopped walking, she had too – and I watched her as she said the word. It was like the word was fragile, sort of precious, and if she didn't say it like that it would break.

'Tobago?' She nodded, and didn't say anything else. She wasn't crying any longer, but she held her head down; her braids and ribbons stuck up and out over her neck. I had never in my life seen such big, shiny ribbons, and never on anybody's hair. I didn't like her being so quiet, it made me feel worried. When she was crying, I felt I could help, but now she was so quiet I felt a little afraid. I wanted to ask her questions, about Tobago, and her gran, but felt I shouldn't. I could hear my mother's voice: 'Don't ask so many questions Margaret. It's rude!' I decided it wasn't a good time to be rude. Instead I said to her, 'Know how to make angels?' She looked at me with a quick sideways glance – I think she was looking to see if I was making fun of her. I wasn't, so she shook her head. I dropped to the ground, on my back, quickly moved my arms up and down in the snow, opened and closed my legs a couple of times, then stood up and pointed. 'See,' I said, 'an angel!'

'Look at dat!' she said. 'It just like dose Christmas cards Gran use to get from Canada and England. It an angel for true. Me want make one too.' She flung herself laughing on to the snow-bank, and began moving her arms and legs like she had just seen me do. That was how our friendship got started – making angels in the snow.

Zulma was my ab-so-lute friend. I had had one other ab-so-lute friend before this, but she had moved away just before last Christmas – to Alberta. After she left, I used to hang out quite a bit with Ti-cush, but she would get so down about *everything*, it was too much sometimes.

I mean *she* didn't have a 'too-too-pretty' sister (that's what my father calls her, 'my too-too-pretty girl'); it was only her and her mother, just the two of them and she didn't have to share her mother with anyone, but they still didn't get along. Of course I *always* took Ti-cush's side – parents could be too-too-difficult sometimes, like my mother going and buying me North Star sneakers. Nobody, but nobody, wears North Stars, but she has to go and buy me North Stars. I refused to wear them; she yelled at me, then my father yelled at me, then they both yelled at me about poverty and poor, starving children. I told them to send the North Stars to those poor starving children – they needed them more than I did; they could even eat them for all I cared. I didn't really mean that, but I was so fed up with my parents going on and on at me.

So I got grounded again for – 'Rudeness to Your Parents' – which has got to be one of the worst, if not *the* worst sin in my house, and God knows there are a lot of them – sins I mean – in my house. My father, of course, or HE as I call HIM, didn't lose the chance to tell me that I needed to be sent back to the West Indies for some 'Good West Indian Discipline'.

2

After making angels in the snow, Zulma and I hung out together a lot, which really bugged Ti-cush. She didn't like Zulma, that was clear. She said she thought Zulma was just a dumb island kid. She was jealous because I wasn't spending as much time with her. I was spending less time with her, not only because I had a new friend, but because I didn't like the way she talked about Zulma. One day I asked her who she was to call anybody a dumb island kid. Her father was from the islands, she told me so herself, and so were my parents. 'How come,' I asked her, 'you talk about Zulma like that? You get upset when people say you're a Newfie from "down east", and you don't like it, so why are you doing it to someone else?' That shut her up, for a while at least, but she didn't like Zulma any better.

Zulma really didn't know much about anything – about living and going to school in Toronto, I mean. Like she didn't even know what a transfer was and was paying twice, sometimes three times to get round on the buses and subways. I set her straight on that one and even showed her how she could make stop-overs on the same transfer, if she was continuing on in the same direction. She knew a lot, and I mean a lot, about Tobago and things like the mango season; why it was better to plant some crops at full moon and not at new moon; and how to kill a chicken, clean it and season it. None of this was any good to her in Toronto, or at school, so I began looking out for her, making sure other kids didn't push her around.

Most of the time she was unhappy, really unhappy. Her

problems made mine look like nothing. When her mother left the island, Zulma was three and she went to live with her gran. Her mother went back for a visit five years ago and that was the last time Zulma had seen her. In that time her mother had got a new husband, her stepfather, and Zulma did not get along with him. He didn't like her either. There were lots of fights; she missed her gran, and didn't want to be in Canada, especially in the winter! I didn't get along with my parents either, but at least I didn't know anything better or anywhere else, except the bloody icy playground and the streets around my home. But Zulma? She talked of beaches and blue sea, sunshine and coconut trees, and days being so hot the asphalt would melt, and a gran who thought she was the most important person in the world. If I were in her shoes I would have gone mad, or maybe run away, but she didn't. At least she had me.

It was maybe a month after she and I had become friends that the Veep – the Vice-Principal – sent for me. I hadn't been caught throwing snowballs recently so I was pretty sure he wasn't going to bawl me out or put me in the hall, but I was still a little worried. When I got to his office I found Zulma, and Zulma's teacher. She was in the same grade as me but had a different teacher.

My first thought was that Zulma was in trouble but I was wrong. Mr Dunkirk explained to me that she was really upset about something but that neither he nor her teacher could get anything from her. He knew I was good friends with her, he said, so maybe I could find out so that they could help her. He cleared his throat when he finished speaking, then said, 'Well then, well then.' He looked at me, then at Zulma's teacher, cleared his throat again and got up and left. Zulma's teacher followed him. I laughed to myself and thought how strange adults were.

I was sitting next to Zulma. She was hunched over in her chair with her head down, and she was kicking her right sneaker against the tiled floor making a sort of squeaky noise.

8

'Hey can I give you my North Stars to do that with? I really hate them.' She looked over at me and giggled. I smiled. 'So, what's up?'

'Nothing.'

'Nothing's why the Veep sent for me, right? C'mon Zulma, tell me what's up? You know I won't talk if you don't want me to.'

'It's not that.'

'Well what is it then?'

When she began to talk, it was so low I couldn't hear her properly. 'Me a get . . . one letter . . .' I pulled my chair in closer, 'from me ggg . . . gran . . . last night. She say . . . she say . . . she mmiss me . . .' She was crying, her tears dropping on to her skirt. 'She say . . . she does . . . ddream . . . every night . . . about me, how me crying and not happy.' Her right hand was doing the same thing it did the day I first saw her in the playground, she was wiping it up and down her skirt. I put my arm around her shoulders, like I did that day in the playground. 'Me miss she too, Margaret . . . bad bad . . . de goats and de chickens dem . . . and de sun and . . .'

'Zulma' – I don't know why but I was whispering – 'Zulma,' I said again, 'I promise you, by the end of the year you will be back in Tobago. I promise I'll get you there.' Why I said what I said I still don't know, except that I just wanted to help her, and didn't like to see her sad. I believed my promise though. We both believed my promise. I had no money; I didn't know how I was going to help her to get back to Tobago without money, but I was the only person who wanted to help her. We didn't talk about it any more, but it was there between us.

When I talked to Mr Dunkirk later on – Zulma didn't want to stay and talk to him – he came over all hearty and talked about homesickness and how homesickness always passed. 'Homesickness!' I wanted to say. 'Homesickness! How can you talk about homesickness?' The things adults do with words, like my mother and Rudeness, or my father and Coloured People.

9

When they get through with the words, they've lost all meaning. That was what Mr Dunkirk was doing with the word 'homesickness'; it was really stretching it to its limit to take in what Zulma was feeling, and the last time he said it, 'homesickness', I felt it burst and collapse. There was no word I knew of that described what Zulma felt, except maybe plain old loss – loss, loss, loss, and even that word left out a lot. Anyway I left as quickly as I could without committing my mother's sin of rudeness.

I'm pretty sure it was on the way home that day (I had asked Zulma to spend the night at my place) that I began to learn Tobago-talk from Zulma.

When I first met Zulma, I didn't understand much of what she said, especially when she talked quickly, which was often. Within two or three weeks though, I was understanding most of what she was saying. Her talk had all these hills and valleys – nothing like my flat, old, boring Canadian talk. Where I would say I, she would say me, or ah; where I said her, she would say she; but that was only the beginning of how we talked differently, although it was supposed to be English we both spoke.

When I asked her on the way home that evening to teach me Tobago-talk (that was what I called it), she got all quiet and serious; she didn't say anything for a while. Then: 'Is what you want to talk like that for? You speak nice already.'

'I like the way you talk. I want to talk like that. Sometimes I hear my mother on the phone with her Jamaican friends; when they get going I can hardly understand them.'

'Your mother talk dialect?'

'Yep, but she likes to pretend she doesn't know how to; she thinks it's better to sound like a Canadian. In any case, after a while you begin to lose your accent you know, like you're doing.' I nudged her and smiled.

'Me? Never! Me never going lose me accent. I'se a Tobagonian and I'se proud of it.'

'All right, all right, I'm sorry.' I laughed. 'I didn't mean to

10

insult you.' It was real important to Zulma to believe in where she came from and who she was – Tobagonian. I had forgotten that. To say she was sounding less Tobagonian might mean she was growing away from her gran and Tobago. Her gran might not understand her. Yet I knew she liked her classes where she learned English, what I called flat English or plain English, no hills or valleys.

'Well, I want to talk like you . . . if you'll teach me.'

'You serious?'

'Uh huh, then I'll be bilingual.'

'Oh all right. When you want start?'

'Now, how would you say, "I want to go to the movies"?'

'Me a want go to de movies.'

'Me a want go to the movies.'

'No, not *the* but *de*, de movies.'

That was how our lessons in Tobago-talk started. She never said anything, but I knew that Zulma was very proud to be teaching me her talk. I was always telling her stuff, and explaining to her how things went, like why it was important for her not to ever wear those blue, satin ribbons again; but now she could teach me something. When we did our lessons in Tobago-talk, she looked really happy.

One day we had a lesson in swear words. She taught me the ones they used in Tobago; I taught her the ones we used in Canada. I even threw in some Italian and Greek swear words that my friends Franca and Penny had taught me. Most of her words were like ours, but Zulma could put them together in real interesting ways like I had never heard before. She had learnt it from listening to a neighbour back home in Tobago who, Zulma said, cursed like a real artist. Her gran would chase her inside if she saw her hanging about listening to Elvie cussing – that was how Zulma called it – not cursing, but cussing. She would press her ear up to the wall to hear what Elvie was saying, and since the walls were thin you could hear real well. Sometimes (it depended on where her gran was) she would even try and sneak back outside to hear Elvie cuss, it was so

11

beautiful. We laughed so much that day. If her gran were to hear her saying these words, Zulma said, she would wash her mouth out with soap and hang it out to dry. That broke us up again. It was one of the best lessons we had – learning swear words.

3

My father is always telling me I should do my homework in my room so I can 'concentrate better'. I like the kitchen, it's warm (it's got a nice red tiled floor), and has a friendly feeling. My mother likes to iron there as well, not in the basement like my father would like her to, and I like to sit there and talk to her sometimes.

I was sitting in the kitchen one evening doing my homework and thinking about swearing, it must have been right after our swearing lesson. Why else would I have been thinking about swearing? My mother didn't think it was proper to swear, even words like damn and blasted which you hear on T.V. all the time – she says these words are too heavy for my tongue to lift up. So as I was sitting there thinking about this and figuring out my maths problem, I said to my mum: 'Look Mum – damn, blasted, shit, see – my tongue can lift them up. It's real easy too.' She got all righteous with me and sent me up to my room to finish my homework. That is what I don't understand about adults, how when you show them they're wrong they always punish you for their mistake. All I was doing was showing her I could use those words and the world wouldn't come to an end. Also I don't really think any word is good or bad – it's what you do with it and how you use it.

But my mother? She doesn't know any better, after all she does live with HIM. On a scale of one to ten I would give her a five, and maybe another three points for sympathy, for living with Him. Him, I would give a minus ten. A lot of the time I feel sorry for my mum; she lets my father push her around too much. She fights back sometimes but not often enough. There are times when I want to take her and shake her and say: 'Stand up for yourself.' Like the Bob Marley song: *Get up, stand up, stand up for your rights*. I'm sure she would pretend she had never heard of Bob Marley; my father, of course, would say he was a disgrace to black people. No, he would never say black but Coloured People, capital C, capital P.

Some people – I don't know who, and don't care to know either – might say I had nothing to complain about, but I think I do. My mum thinks that because I am a girl, I should like to dress up and wear make-up, like my sister; that I should always be polite and not swear or curse. I say to her, 'Look Mum, if someone calls you a name like nigger, what d'you want me to do? Say excuse me, you shouldn't say that? No way, I tell them exactly where to go,' and when I tell her where that is, she gets pissed off with me and sends me to my room.

I discovered a word a few days ago – neurotic – I looked it up in the dictionary; and that's what I think my mother is – neurotic. My father, on the other hand, is a male chauvinist pig, no doubt about that. That's what I mean about having problems with parents: one a neurotic, the other a male chauvinist pig. I mean like why else would my mother always be buying things, we don't need half the things she buys but she still buys them. If you go in our basement you'll find three sewing machines, four electric irons, three toasters and on and on; and these aren't new things, she buys them all at second-hand stores, but we don't need them.

Sometimes she and my father fight about it, then she calls the Goodwill, or Salvation Army, and they come and pick up some of the things. And beds, beds she buys new; it seems like every year one of us gets a new one. She has this thing about beds; I think it must be because she was really poor when she was a child. She doesn't talk about it much but every so often my father, the MCP, brings it up to show HOW FAR WE HAVE COME. She just sits there and lets him go on and on about how she doesn't want to remember how poor she was; how she didn't

14

have a bed to sleep on and would often only have sweetened water for lunch.

Sometimes though, especially when he's not around, she can be real nice; then I can get her to braid my hair. She really doesn't like to do it – braid my hair – she thinks it's kind of lower class. Only poor people, she says, would corn row their hair, and no matter how many *Essence* magazines I show her, with these super cool black women wearing braids, she just sucks her teeth and says it's all foolishness, that 'straightened hair is so much better'. Of course my sister, Jo-Ann, the Chub Queen herself, has *her* hair straightened with all kinds of gunk. One day though, I even got Mum to braid my hair *and* Zulma's – we were like two African princesses, except my skin wasn't dark enough. I wish I had Zulma's kind of dark black skin, it's just like velvet, and with her long braids – ooh she was beautiful . . .

I wish my mum would stick up for me more though, with my father. He's always trying to push me around – not physically, but he's always on at me about something: how I'm not like Jo-Ann (thank God); how I'm too rude; and how I need some Good West Indian Discipline, in capitals of course. There are a lot of capitals around my house – Rudeness, Coloured People, Punctuality, Respect for Adults, and on and on.

One day I got so fed up with him going on about Good West Indian Discipline, I said to him: 'Dad, you're always talking about Good West Indian Discipline, what is Bad West Indian Discipline?' He gave me this look, like he didn't know if I was being rude or not. Then he made a kind of noise that he makes in his throat – 'Harrumph!' – it's a real gross sound, and he continued eating. I could barely keep from smiling, for once I had shut him up. I took a quick glance at my sister and she was sniggering too.

My father is always going on about HOW IMPORTANT IT IS TO DO WELL AT SCHOOL, and get good grades and all that stuff, because being COLOURED PEOPLE we have to be twice as good to get anywhere – and I believe him. I just wish he wouldn't go on

15

so about it. Once or twice a year would be enough; instead it's like every week we get this lecture. The funny thing is that although I get good marks and am at the top of the class, he still prefers Jo-Ann, who's lucky if she scrapes a fifty average.

Then there's my dear brother, Jonathon, the great Rib-Roast Prime Minister I call him. He's so perrrfect – not half as smart as me, but *he's* going to be a lawyer, my father says. Me, he says, my mouth will get me in trouble. I keep wishing my brother would scrape my father's car – he's just learning to drive – but no such luck. I really don't understand how girls can like him, they're always calling him. He's so lifeless, so perfect. I mean like he won't wear an Afro because that's too street – his words – and punk, of course, horrifies him. He wants his hair cut low like my father's, and he even chews like my father now – like a cow, slow and stupid.

I don't want to say my father is a bad man, he's not. It's just that he is a phoney in a lot of ways, and I can't stand phoneys. The only thing he's got going for him is that he's adult!

He's phoney because he goes on at my mother about how she won't keep her money in the bank – and she won't. She has this 'partners' saving scheme where she and her women friends pool their money and take turns getting it. Every month my mother puts one-hundred dollars into the kitty along with her friends (I think there were nine of them including my mother). One month my mother gets nine-hundred dollars; the next month Daisy gets it, the next month Dorcas, and so on until all nine of them have each got nine-hundred dollars. He, my father, says this is primitive; that she's losing interest; that she has 'got to move into the modern age and leave her past behind her'. He's an accountant with the government, so this really burns him up. But he plays dominoes – he and all these men from the West Indies sit around all day and play this real stupid game.

My mother doesn't like him playing; she says he wastes his Saturdays when he could be helping her. He likes the game, but wishes he didn't like it. I've heard him telling my mother that he has done the best of all the men he plays with; that he thinks it too lower class, but he still plays and goes on at my mum about her 'partners' saving scheme.

That's why I say he's a phoney. He's not leaving *his* past behind him, but he wants her to. And he's *so* concerned about being coloured, which as far as I can see means being stuffy and boring and not liking anything worth liking, like the Wailers or calypso, or even Caribana, our version of Carnival.

4

Like I said before, whenever I think I've got problems, I've only got to think of Zulma and her problems. One day I asked her if she had ever asked her mother to send her back to her gran.

'Plenty time Margaret, plenty time, but she only get sad and start to cry, and say how Momma, that's what she call Gran, going blame she and say she should never have send for me. And she never should.'

'So? What if your gran blames her. You're not happy.'

'Me know, me know, but that's what she say. Me stepfather not going want me to go either.'

'Why? He doesn't like you.'

'He don't want spend de money, although is not his money, is Mammy own. He like having me around to run all kind of errand for he – buying cigarettes and pop; he even have me cleaning he shoes.'

'Damn! damn! damn! Adults! You know I think there should be some kind of exam before people can become adults and have power over other people. Your stepfather and my father would fail, over and over again. We just got to get you some money for a ticket. Your gran doesn't have any?'

'Uh uh. She poor, not poor poor, for we always have plenty food from de garden, and the animals dem, but she don't have much money. If she did have she would have been up here like dat,' Zulma snapped her fingers, 'before cat say miaow, to get me.'

'C'mon,' I said, 'race you to the swings.' I didn't want to get

Zulma all down again, that's why I changed the subject, but I had an idea and I wanted to talk to my mother about it.

My mum had promised to braid my hair that coming Sunday, so when finally HE had gone to bed for his Sunday afternoon nap, she sat down with me to do it.

She sat on the couch; I sat on the rug between her legs, and she started on my hair. The T.V. was on.

'Mum, can I turn off the T.V.? I want to talk to you.'

'What about?'

'About Zulma.'

'Zulma?'

'Yes. Can I turn off the T.V.?'

'Turn it down then.'

'Off Mum, off – I want to talk to you.'

'Oh all right, but I don't see . . . what about Zulma? What d'you want to talk to me about Zulma for?'

I loved nothing better than having my hair combed and braided. It always feels so safe and secure, sitting there and feeling my mum's fingers picking up the hair and tightly braiding the rows. I didn't say anything for a while, I just wanted to enjoy the feeling.

'Margaret, you made me turn off the T.V. What you want to talk about?'

'Hmmm, it just feels so good Mum, when you comb my hair.'

'You should straighten it, like your sister's. Look at this mop – say you wearing it Afro? Is nice strong hair – it would come out real nice straightened, even Jerri curled.'

'Oh Mum, don't let's start that again. I'm me, not fat, slobbo Jo-Ann, and I don't want to straighten my hair.'

'Don't talk about your sister like that.'

'You know Mum, all that stuff she puts in her hair – it affects the brains – that's why she's so stupid.'

'Hush your mouth child, and sit still. Now what about Zulma? You making me miss my show with all your carrying on.'

19

'Mum are you still saving my baby bonus cheques from the government?'

'Yes, why?'

'How much d'you have saved?'

'Not sure, about four-thousand dollars.'

'Is the money mine?'

My mother was quiet for a while. I could feel her concentrating on getting a row to go in a swirl over the top of my head.

'Uh huh . . .'

'So why don't you give it to me?' I knew I had my mum at a bit of a disadvantage because she had to concentrate to do the braids nicely. Although she didn't like braiding my hair, she always liked to do a nice job. My question stopped her and she had to loose out the braid and start all over again. She sucked her teeth, long and loud.

'Give it to you?'

'Yes, give it to me. You said it was mine.'

'Is yours, true, but not to spend like that – is for when you reach eighteen or nineteen – and anyway some of it you can't touch before you twenty.'

'Why?'

'Turn round and let me finish your hair. Your father going to be getting up soon and he going to want his tea.'

'Why can't I get some of it till I'm twenty? That's six years away. Why?'

'Because your godmother said so, that's why, in the will.'

'Godmother? Aunt Agnes? She's alive!'

'Not Aunt Agnes, someone else.'

'Who Mum, who?'

'Mrs Blewchamp. I used to work for her . . .'

'And she's my godmother?'

'Well, yes and no. I call her that though she never come to church and stand up for you, like Aunt Agnes. She used to say she stop believing in God, but she gave you money when you was born and said she was your second mother. I said, "You

20

mean godmother"; she laugh and say no, just a stand-in mother. She liked you best of all the children.'

'When did she die? Why didn't you tell me this before?'

'Just listen to her! Your mouth so full of question Margaret. She died about ten years ago – you were too small to remember her. When I first come to Canada I used to work for her, she was even old back then, and lonely.'

'Where was her family?'

'If you don't sit still, you not going to have corn rows Margaret – you going have zig zag rows.'

'Sorry Mum, but you just telling the story so slowly. Can't you talk faster?'

'My tongue moving as fast as I can move it Margaret. You too rude child, I keep telling you that.'

'Mum – Mrs – what's her name?'

'Harriet – Harriet Blewchamp.'

'Where was her family? Didn't she have any children of her own?'

'I don't know; either moved away or dead. She never told me much, in words that is, but her eyes used to talk a lot. You just had to look at them and know that she had seen some bad times, real bad times . . . well at least I could see it. If she had any family here in Toronto, they never bothered with her. When I started to work for her, she wanted someone to live in, help her in the house. Your father was studying and I had to work to make ends meet, so I moved in with her – only during the week. She used to have someone else on weekends. I worked with her for three, maybe four years. She liked me, I liked her, and she never treated me anyway funny.'

'What d'you mean funny?'

'Well, you know some white people can be real funny with you. Is not good enough that you working for them, but they like to act like they own your soul and despise you at the same time.'

My mother's voice got rough when she said this. I looked up

21

quickly at her face – she was frowning. 'Ouch!' I said. My mum had yanked the piece of hair she was holding, 'That hurt Mum.'

'Sorry, but you keep turning your head this way and that, and moving it all over the place.'

'Please go on Mum.'

'Anyway, even after I stopped working with her, I used to go and look for her – especially at Easter and Christmas. Sometimes I even used to bring her over to our place; Cuthbert would go and get her in the car. I never liked thinking of her alone in that big old house when everybody else had family. She never used to complain though.

'When each one of you was born, she would come and see me and say she would stand by you – she give each one of you money when you born. She use to want to hold each one of you when you born; her hands was all twist up with arthritis but she would hold you and get this funny, funny look on her face – like she going to cry – but she was happy. Then this far-away look would come in her eyes, and sometimes she would talk to herself real low.

'She always say she was going to leave something for you all. I never believe her, that she would leave something. For one thing she never look rich to me, but she did keep her word. Each one of you got something from her, and you she left some papers and books.'

'Me? Why me?'

'Don't ask me, she took a real liking to you. Said you reminded her of herself and she used to use a word to describe you – feisty – that sound very much like what I always say you acting like – faysty. I asked her once and they mean the same thing. Strange, from the first day she lay eyes on you in the hospital she like you. She even ask me to call you Harriet, her name, but Cuthbert wanted Margaret, his mother's name. She used to call you Harriet though. Hold on, I'm almost done.'

'So, go on, what else?'

'Not much else. She left you all about fifteen-hundred dollars each when she died.'

'Is that all you know about her though?'

'Uh huh. A friend of mine who used to work for someone who knew her said she was in the war and escaped.'

'You mean she was a spy?'

'Don't think so – go and get me some hairpins, and hurry.'

I came back with the hairpins real quick.

'Well if she wasn't a spy, what was she escaping from?'

'I don't know Margaret. She had some numbers tattooed on her wrist that my friend said was connected with the war, but she never talked about it.'

'Numbers! She must have been Jewish, Mum – those numbers mean she was in a concentration camp.'

'I don't know Margaret. C'mon turn around. I went to her funeral, there was hardly anybody there, and I was the only coloured person. I still remember how strange I felt. This old man came up to me – he was important looking – had white, white hair and was very handsome. He was crying; I had never seen a man cry before or since. He came over and introduced himself and say Harriet – Mrs Blewchamp – had told him all about me, and how happy he was to meet someone who was kind to her.'

'So when did you get the money?'

'I didn't get the money, I mean your money. A lawyer sent to call me, said it was about Mrs Blewchamp's will.'

'Did you go?'

'Yes. I was really nervous, but to cut a long story short, he told me she left each one of you fifteen-hundred dollars, me twenty-five-hundred dollars, and you her papers and books.'

'Jeez, I wish I knew her. So why can't I get the money?'

'Because that's what the will says – the papers and books you get when you're sixteen or seventeen. There. I'm all done. You said you wanted to talk about Zulma.' I nodded.

'Mum, why can't I have some of the baby bonus money for Zulma to buy her a ticket to go back home – to Tobago?'

'Zulma's home is here now Margaret . . .'

'But Mum she's real unhappy, and just like Mrs Blewchamp

was kind to us, can't we be kind to Zulma? Please Mum, it's not a lot – four-hundred and fifty-five dollars.'

'How d'you know that?'

'I called the airlines and asked. Look Mum her stepfather hates her, her mother's kind of scared of him, and Zulma wants to be home with her gran – please.'

'I don't believe in getting involved in other people's business.'

'Other people's business? She's my friend – she's like my sister. No, she's more than my sister, she's not "other people", and it's *my* money – you said it was and I want it.'

'You better watch your mouth child . . .'

'But *I* need that money, to help my friend. How come I don't have any rights over what is *my* money?'

'Because *I* am your mother and *I* decide *when* and *how* you get it, and that's that.'

'But that's not fair!' I was crying now. 'It's not fair – you go spending all kinds of stupid money on clothes for Jo-Ann and make-up and all kinds of junk we don't need, and you won't give me any of my own money to help my friend. I hate you, I hate this family!'

I saw this look come over my mother's face, real anger and hurt; she raised her hand to slap me but just then HE came into the living-room.

'Sorry Mum,' I muttered, turned and left the room quickly, knowing when I was beaten. At least for the time being. As I left I could hear his voice going on about 'that child being too rude'.

I went up to my room and looked at myself in the mirror. Not even my braids could make me feel better, it just wasn't fair, the power adults had. I stuck my tongue out at myself, threw myself across the bed and drummed my heels on the wall until my mother yelled at me to stop it.

5

For the next week or so I was mad as hell. I refused to talk to anyone at home. I said good morning and good evening, and that was it. I was still burning from the unfairness of my mother – her refusal to help me help Zulma, but I was also excited about what she had told me about my 'godmother'.

Out of everyone else she had liked me best and that was real important to me. Families are O.K. – sometimes better than O.K., though mine hasn't been that way for a long time, but you have to like whoever you're stuck with in a family. I'm supposed to love my sister, the Chub Queen, my brother, the Rib Roast Prime Minister, my mother *and* my father, and I suppose I do love them. I mean I would help them if they were in trouble, but I don't often like them – maybe except my mum. Zulma I love and like, she's closer to me than my own sister; and Mrs Blewchamp, who was no relative of mine, liked me and thought I was special – she was even white.

Maybe it was then I first started thinking of changing my name, from boring old Margaret, to Harriet. Mrs Blewchamp had really lived, she was in the war, in a concentration camp, and had escaped and she wanted *me* to have her name. I mean, like who was Margaret? My father's mother, whom I didn't really know, and didn't like, because HE was always threatening to send me to her for some Good West Indian Discipline.

I do know that that was when I made my list:
THINGS I WOULD MOST LIKE TO SEE CHANGED IN MY LIFE.
   1. My father. I want a different father, or no father at all.

25

2. My mother's attitude. My mother has an attitude, a real problem, she won't stick up for me or for herself.
3. Zulma's life. It would be the end of the world, for me, if she went back to Tobago, but I would like her to be happy and she will only be happy there.
4. My sister. My sister should gain another 50lbs; I would love her even more because she would be *so* unhappy and I would have to feel sorry for her. She wouldn't be so pretty either.
5. My skin. At least five shades darker, like Zulma's, and braids like hers. Right now I'm too in between, like the colour of mud – brown mud. (How come Jo-Ann's called cinnamon?)
6. My name. I want a name that means something – important?
7. My brother. An outbreak of pimples.

Then I drew up another list:
THINGS TO DO TO MAKE THOSE CHANGES
1. Send my father away – far away – for some Good West Indian Discipline? Ha, ha. Impossible – must learn to tune him out more.
2. My mother must get a job. She has worked before, but HE won't let her, says she should be home for us children. HE means HIMSELF of course. She's always happier when she's working, though she buys more junk. I will try and find her a job. How can I make her stick up more for me????? Agree to have my hair straightened?? No way!
3. Zulma: pray. Never hurts to try everything, although I don't really believe God – He or She – ever listens. Much too busy with more important problems. Get a job to earn money for her fare? Run a marathon? Walk across Canada? Maybe, maybe. That would get them, I could see the headlines: GIRLS WALKING ACROSS CANADA TO RAISE MONEY TO GO HOME. I could carry a sign: HELP ZULMA GO HOME TO GRAN or HOME TO GRAN. Sounds great, won't

26

work though. The adults would probably stop us, but something MUST BE DONE.

4. Chub Queen – buy her chocolates, chips and Coke. She loves them.
5. Can't change my skin or the length of my hair, but I do have some nice things about me – my eyes. I like the way they slant and sparkle. My mother says it's because we have Carib Indian in us, but she won't say more than that, so maybe I have a great, great, great, great-grandmother who was Carib, with eyes like mine. I've got good teeth and a nice smile, so I've been told. Don't feel there's much to smile or show my teeth about though.
6. My name. Go to the library and look up famous women to see what their names were. Maybe I could change my name. I'm sure HE would never let me.

That was how it happened that me, Ti-cush (believe it or not) and Zulma happened to be walking along St Clair on a Saturday afternoon. We were on our way to the library. I wanted to check out famous women and to get some books for a music project for school.

Ti-cush had got a little friendlier with Zulma and we had been hanging out together.

'Hey guys,' I said, 'can you imagine being killed "in the line of duty"?' I dropped my voice on the last words, 'and getting medals after you die? That would be real exciting wouldn't it? I think I would like to be a spy.'

'Once you're dead,' Ti-cush said, her voice real dry, 'you're dead, you've got no way of knowing whether or not you've got a medal. What d'you want to die for? It's boring, painful as hell I'm sure and I hate pain – I can't stand it.' She gave a little shudder, all for effect, as she said this. 'You know when I get my period I just have to go to bed and take pills. It's terrible. My mother says I have a very low pain threshold.'

I didn't say anything. I didn't want to start Ti-cush on her period. She could go on forever on that. I hadn't started mine yet and never felt I could say anything anyway. Zulma would *never* talk about hers. If I asked her something direct she would answer, but she would never go on like Ti-cush. But then everything was a problem for Ti-cush and she loved being the centre of attention.

After a while I went on: 'Well I wouldn't want to be tortured, I'd want to be killed quickly so I didn't have to feel any pain. If I were a spy, I would have cyanide capsules in a false tooth that I could bite on – I saw that on T.V. I would die immediately. That way I wouldn't be tortured and I wouldn't have to give away my country's secrets. I read something about a woman like that; her name was Mata Hari, she used to dance naked in clubs and had a lot of boy-friends.'

'She have a cyanide tablet?' Zulma asked.

'No, they made her stand against a wall and soldiers shot her.'

'And you think *that's* exciting?' Ti-cush said. 'You're sick, that's what. It's gross and depressing, all this talk of dying and soldiers.'

'Haven't you ever thought of what it must be like to die . . . I mean what it must feel like?' I asked her. 'Not the pain, but just the feeling. It's really too bad people can't come back and tell you what it's all about.'

'Ghosts!' Zulma said. 'You talking 'bout ghosts, dead people coming back to talk to you!' Ti-cush was looking real angry now and I began to laugh.

'God, both of you are real depressing, first death and cyanide and now ghosts,' she said.

'Me gran use to tell me plenty of ghost story, and some of dem real funny. You want me tell you guys some?'

I could see Ti-cush getting all sullen and pouty, so I told Zulma she could tell us some other time – 'like when we're in bed. I love feeling scared when I'm safe,' I said.

'O.K.,' she said, 'the next time me sleep over – right?'

'Right.' I laughed. 'So what would you like to be Ti-cush? I said I wanted to be a spy.'

Ti-cush didn't say anything for a while, then: 'I'd like to be a queen, with lots of fancy clothes and servants and money, and . . . lots of boy-friends.' You could tell from her tone and attitude, sort of angry and defiant, that she expected us to challenge her. We did. Zulma jumped in first with both feet.

'But Ti-cush, queens don't have boy-friends. Me mean queens does have kings, right Margaret?'

Before I could answer, Ti-cush said, 'Well a movie star then.'

Zulma jumped in again. 'Me think you better off being a movie star, because me read where a lot of dose queen get dey head chop off, and dat must be real painful – having some big chopper come chopping down on your neck. What if de blade dull, like when me gran was trying to chop off de neck of dis chicken – it was an old cock. Lord, you never see so much sawing back and forth to chop off dat poor old fowl neck. If you can't stand pain, me say a movie star make a lot more sense, Ti-cush.'

I was watching Ti-cush's face as Zulma went on – it got more and more – the only word I have to describe it is growly. She is quite light-skinned for a black person (what my mother calls red-skin) and her face got sort of fatter and redder and growly as Zulma talked. When Zulma got to the part about her gran sawing the chicken's neck, Ti-cush covered her ears. When Zelma was done, she turned to her and spat the words out:

'When I want your stupid opinion, I'll ask for it. Otherwise shut to hell up about you and your stupid gran.'

'Hey c'mon Ti-cush,' I said, 'that's nasty and mean. Zulma was only trying to help.' I looked at Zulma and I could tell she was angry and hurt, but before I could say anything to her Ti-cush told her she was sorry.

'Look Zulma, don't take it personally – I've got some things on my mind.'

'Now Zulma,' I said, 'your turn. Who do you want to be?'

'You guys ever hear about Angela Davis?' She didn't give us a chance to answer, but she rushed on. 'Me gran use to tell me about she, how she fight for black people, and how she had to run for she life. Gran had pictures of she stick up over she bed and me bed – me still remember de Afro she used to wear – it was de biggest Afro me did ever see on anybody. Me use to ask Gran to tell me 'bout she every night, before me go to bed. Gran say de police frame she because dey didn't like she fighting for she people – black people in de United States – and dat it remind she of some of de stories she use to hear about slavery time. How de owners use to always try and kill or maim people who try and help other slaves. And you know what, me have one of dose pictures with me. When me coming away me ask Gran if me could have it and she let me bring it with me. Me have it up over me bed now, and dat is who me would like to be – somebody like Angela Davis . . . and fight for so something real important.'

By the time she was done, we were standing outside the library; we were all quiet – I don't know why – thinking about Angela Davis (at least I was) and what Zulma had just said.

I got some great books on reggae music and Rastafarians for my music project; one on Mata Hari, and two on Harriet Tubman. When the librarian gave me a list of famous women with Harriet Tubman's name on it, I remembered I had learnt something about her in my Black Heritage class; that she had helped slaves escape from the States to Canada. She had the same name as Harriet Blewchamp – that made me feel good – like I was on the right track or something.

By the time I got through at the library though, I knew I was going to be half an hour late for supper.

'HE is going to be mad as hell with me,' I said. They understood. 'You know what guys,' I went on, 'the world would be such a fun place without certain adults – like parents – my parents.' We all laughed. 'We should form a group: WORLD WITHOUT PARENTS – WWP – or WAP – world after parents; recruit other kids to the cause.' That really broke us up.

6

I was right outside the McDonald's when the thought hit me. Looking back, that probably had something to do with it, the McDonald's I mean. I had been running, I was tired, and I was late – now forty-five minutes late – and I was sick and tired of being scared of my father and his power. I'm already in trouble, I thought, and whether I was a half-hour, forty-five minutes, or one hour late, it was the same trouble, so what the hell, I was going to live dangerously. A big chocolate milk-shake seemed dangerous enough, so I went into McDonald's and ordered the biggest milk-shake they had. It only cost one dollar and fifty cents, but it was the most expensive milk-shake I had ever had. I paid for it in other ways.

While I had my shake I looked at my books. On the back of one of the Tubman books was a picture of Harriet Tubman; for someone who lived dangerously she looked quite harmless. I don't know what I was expecting, but it wasn't the calm strong face that stared back at me from the cover – and plain too. The eyes though, looked like they had seen things; maybe this was what my mother meant when she talked of Mrs Blewchamp's eyes – like they had seen things. Would I trust my life to this woman? I stared at the face, stroked the picture . . . yes, yes I would. I would trust her.

I flicked through the book on Mata Hari – there were even some pictures inside – one of her being shot by a firing-squad, another of her dancing. She was just about naked in the dancing picture, with bracelets on her upper arms. I stared and stared at her breasts and hips: maybe one day, I thought, I'm going to have breasts and hips like this. I was still pretty flat all over. Chub Queen Jo-Ann was the one with the curves in my family. I worried a lot about those things – couldn't talk to anyone about them. I knew I didn't want to look like my mother, her breasts were too big and heavy; all I could think was that they would get in the way and be like weights around my neck. It was like everything was weight on my mum, even her body – no, I didn't want that. I didn't want to be fat like Jo-Ann either, she was too much like my mother; her breasts were already humungous. Maybe I wouldn't have any breasts at all. Sometimes I thought that would be great, nothing to worry about. But then how would people know I was a girl? Zulma was wearing a bra already, size thirty-four cup, she told me, and I still didn't have much of anything. There were a couple times when people even thought I was a boy – from behind – especially with my Afro. Well I wasn't going to pad and stuff my bra like I knew Ti-cush did (she told me so herself). It wasn't important enough to me, not yet at least.

I was one hour and fifteen minutes late, and I was going to be cool about it. Jo-Ann opened the door all smiles, and whispered: 'You're going to get it.'

'Buzz off Chub Queen.'

'I'll get you for that,' she said. 'Just wait.'

'I'm waiting.'

I washed my hands, and slid into my seat at the dining-table. Everyone had just about finished eating. 'Evening Mum, evening Dad. Sorry I'm late.'

Silence. My mother got up and got my plate and put it in front of me. She began to clear the empty plates and dishes off the table. I was glad for the noise she made with the dishes and cutlery as she stacked them; it provided a sort of cover for me and I made myself as small as possible as I ate. I wasn't very hungry because of the milk-shake but I didn't want to call attention to myself by leaving or refusing food.

Suddenly, HE makes this gross sound in his throat: 'Harrumph!' and I jump, and my knife falls to the floor – talk about being uncool. I bend to pick it up.

'So what's the excuse this time young lady?' He always calls me young lady when he's going to heavy me out. 'This is the third time this week you've been late.'

'No excuse Dad. I forgot the time and stayed too long at the library.'

He made the gross sound in his throat again and began on The Importance of Coloured People Being on Time – I began to tune him out. The last words I heard were, 'People think that all Coloured People are always late'. I had heard the lecture a million times; it was no use interrupting or talking back, he just went on and on. My defence was to shut him out, think of something I liked – a book I was reading, a tune from the Wailers, anything – and every so often say: 'Yes Dad, yes Dad'. He *always* mentioned that life was *so much better in Barbados* where children were children and taught to be polite, punctual and respectful of adults. He would finish off the whole thing by saying that that was what I needed – some Good West Indian Discipline.

I had to be real careful with this plan of mine: once I had tuned him out so much, I hadn't heard him ask me if I thought he was a fool. I made my usual 'Yes Dad' reply, and suddenly I knew I had said something wrong. *Everyone* was super quiet at the table including my father, and he *never* stops during his 'little talks'. I didn't know what he had said. I knew that I had said, 'Yes Dad.' All I could think of to do was say, 'No Dad', and see if that worked. It did – it was like pushing a button – he cleared his throat again and continued. It was my sister who later told me what he had said. We both cracked up laughing; she can be fun sometimes, Jo-Ann. Ever since then I've been very careful to mutter my answers so HE can't quite make out what I'm saying – I hope!

Anyway, when he was all done talking, he grounded me for a week – the longest time ever – but I had had my milk-shake and was feeling pretty good about taking my time coming home. For the first time, I hadn't let my fear of my father stop me doing what I wanted to do, and it felt good even though I was grounded. In any case, I had two projects to do, and I could use the time.

When I finished eating, my mum told me and my sister she wanted us to help her wash up the dishes and tidy up the kitchen.

'How come HE,' I asked, pointing to my brother, 'never gets to do any work around here? I don't see my name on these dishes or on this floor. His hands don't seem broken to me.'

My mother told me to shut up, that he was a boy, and that he had better things to do.

'Like what?' I said. 'How come he doesn't have better things to do than eat? I've got homework to do just like he does – so why can't he do housework? My teacher says men can do jobs women do, and women can do jobs like welding and construction. So why can't he do the dishes, Mum?'

'You hear what you sound like? A real street woman. You always have to carry on about everything.'

'But I have to carry on, Mum – I've got homework and he's got homework. Dad expects us all to do well at school – except for her, of course,' I said, throwing a nasty look Jo-Ann's way. 'In any case she couldn't do well even if she tried.'

'You're just jealous,' the fat one said.

'I'm going to call your father for both of you.' That was my mother for you, always having to get HIM involved. She could never settle anything on her own.

'Jo-Ann you go downstairs,' she said, 'and start folding the clean clothes.' My sister started whining. 'Aw Mum, you know I don't like doing that.'

'Just think of your new make-up,' I taunted her. Fatso stuck out her tongue at me as she went, and I gave her the finger – behind my mother's back of course.

'Hey Mum!' Jo-Ann yelled. 'Did you see what she just did?'

My mother ignored her and told me to get to work washing

the dishes. The rest of the evening I spent up in my room, reading about Harriet Tubman and Mata Hari, until I fell asleep. My mum tried waking me once to get me to clean my teeth; I refused to get up. I just lay there playing dead.

7

I could hear the dogs barking in the distance and I was scared, real scared. I was wearing glasses and had dropped them. I couldn't stop and look for them, I could hear the dogs coming closer and closer but I couldn't see where I was going. Suddenly I could see Harriet Tubman's dress – her skirt – it had her face on it: the same face I had seen on the cover of the book. All I had to do was follow it. The face was smiling now, but I could still hear the dogs. Suddenly I was climbing these trees with Harriet and some other slaves – really tall trees. When I looked down, there was Mata Hari – naked, with a real live snake around her arm. She was climbing the tree too.

I stood against a wall facing a firing squad except that there weren't any soldiers: just my parents, Zulma's parents and Ti-cush's mother. They didn't have guns but each was holding a piece of paper with my name written on it. I screamed at them: 'My name is not Margaret, it's . . .' but each time I tried to say my name nothing came out, and I would have to start all over again, screaming: 'My name's not Margaret, it's . . .'

'Margaret! Margaret!'

'No! No! No! not . . .'

'Margaret! Wake up, wake up – what's wrong with you?'

I opened my eyes and shut them quickly – the overhead light was blinding. My mother was standing next to me as I lay on the top bunk. 'What were you dreaming about? You were yelling your head off.'

'Oh nothing.' I rolled over real quick. 'Nothing you'd understand anyway.' My mother stroked my back for a few minutes, I wished she'd go away but I liked her doing it. Then she stopped, turned off the light and left.

This was the first dream I had had about Harriet Tubman. I was going to have a lot more. Some I remembered, some I didn't, but I began to feel really close to her – like I knew her. The morning after the night I had the first dream, I lay in bed thinking about what I had read the night before. I also thought about the dream, and imagined myself a spy, dressing up in disguise and having secret codes. But who would I spy on? I asked myself. My sister? She didn't have any secrets worth spying on, except maybe when she met her boyfriend. She wasn't supposed to have boyfriends, or date – not at least until she was sixteen – HIS ORDERS. I knew for a fact she had been talking to this guy and she may have gone to a movie with him. I was going to keep close tabs on her.

As for Rib Roast, there was even less. In any case, my father would never believe anything about him, even if I showed him the evidence. Maybe I could plant some cigarettes on him and arrange for them to fall out when HE was around. HE would probably say he was just being a man.

What we needed was a war – a teeny-weeny war so I could get in action. But with my luck it would turn into a nuclear war, and we would all be wiped out, spies and all.

Harriet Tubman. Now she was a sort of spy too, but her work was even more scary. She had to take care of people: babies, children, men and women – she had to bring them all the way up to Canada, and not get caught. She was carrying secrets too, a different kind of secret – people; and we didn't need a war for this either. Funny she had all those fainting spells, I thought. Harriet, Harriet Tubman, Harriet Blewchamp, again I thought of changing my name to one that meant something – like Harriet. Harriet Tubman was brave and strong and she was black like me. I think it was the first time I thought of wanting to be called Harriet – I wanted to *be* Harriet.

I could hear my mother calling me: I knew why, to go to

church, but I pretended not to hear. Finally she came to my room and told me it was time to get up and go to church.

'I'm grounded, remember. I'm not supposed to leave the house.'

'You still have to go to church,' was all she said. I could hear my stupid sister laughing in her room. I was still wearing my clothes from the day before. I looked around my room and wondered whether Harriet would have had a room like this. My mother was dying to get her hands on it and make it over 'like Jo-Ann's', all pink and white. I kept telling her I liked it the way it was. Pukey was Jo-Ann's word for my room. Whenever she said this to me, I agreed with her: 'That's right Jo-Ann, pukey – just like you.' That always got her.

I showered, changed, and put on my new jeans and my 'DON'T BOTHER ME I CAN'T COPE' T-shirt. When I went down for breakfast my mother asked me where I thought I was going.

'To church, where else? You said I had to go.'

'Like that?'

'Like what? These are clean clothes.'

'Yes, but I'm not dead yet, and no one's going to say that Tina Cruickshank don't know how to look after her children, or dress them properly, so go up and change *and* put on a dress. Have a little respect for the house of the Lord.'

I was really tempted to say I thought I lived in the house of the Lord; instead, I put up a fight about wearing a dress:

'Aw Mum, you know I hate wearing dresses. I don't want to wear a dress.'

She was like rock itself: 'Go and put on a dress.'

My mother thinks that when she dies, all hell is going to break loose. I don't know how else to explain her most favourite saying after 'You're too rude and faysty'. 'I'm not dead yet', if my hair doesn't look quite the way *she* wants it to look; 'I'm not dead yet', if my sneakers aren't clean enough; 'I'm not dead yet', if she thinks I look untidy. I don't know what she thinks is going to happen when she dies; that I'll stop bathing and wearing clean clothes? Become a bum?

38

Anyway I got through the boring old service, wearing a hated dress. I managed to sit as far away from my sister as I could. Of course Rib Roast never goes unless he wants to, and of course my mother never makes him go. She and my father go sometimes; very, very sometimes – like once a year, at Christmas or Easter. That's what I mean about adults not being fair – but *every* Sunday, unless I have a real good excuse, I have got to find myself in church, listening to this boring old man talk about the Holy Ghost. I would sneak off and go somewhere else, but slobbo Jo-Ann is always there; she sings in the youth choir and just 'loves the church'. Yuck! Her boyfriend sings in the choir too, I'm sure that's why she loves it so much.

I don't like to go on like this about my problems, especially those I can't change, but I remember this weekend. Apart from being grounded, it was also the weekend when HE threatened once again to send me to Barbados. And we all know what I am supposed to get there: GWID – Good West Indian Discipline.

We were having Sunday supper; the chicken tasted great and my father was eating and not talking. Praise be. I got the wishbone and Jo-Ann wanted to break it with me, so I agreed. I won the wish and she started bugging me to tell her what I wished for, although she knows that to tell means bad luck. I had wished for Zulma to go back home to her gran and I really didn't want to talk about it. She wouldn't give up, just kept bugging me to tell her and finally I did.

'I wished for something for you Jo-Ann.'

'For me? Oh that's great, Margaret, I've been dying for a dress I saw at Le Chateau last week.' She was being all sweet and Jo-Annish. 'Tell me, oh tell me Margaret.'

'I wished for you to gain fifty pounds.' I laughed.

Her face crumpled up, like when you crush a paper cup and I felt like a real jerk. I really hadn't meant to hurt her and I was sorry I had said it, she just kept bugging me so much. She looked like she was going to cry.

'Oh I'm sorry Jo-Ann, forget it. I was just teasing. I didn't really wish that.'

To change the subject and get her mind off the fifty pounds she saw rushing on her like a ten-ton truck, I asked my mum if she would help me with my project on Rastas and reggae music. I really should have known better, for before she could answer – she probably would have said no – HE butted in.

'Did I hear you say you were doing a project on Rastas and reggae music?'

'Yes Dad.' I knew what was coming. I should have kept my big mouth shut, but it was too late. He went on and on about how Rastas were criminal, and how they gave decent, hard-working Coloured People – I wanted to say like Mr Cuthbert Cruickshank, hip, hip hurrah! – a bad name; how they smoked dope, and how their music was primitive. I turned to Mum. 'Say something,' I said, 'you know that's not true, you're from Jamaica.'

'Be quiet when I'm talking,' he said.

'But what you're saying is not true. I've read about them, they're really quite religious. They believe Haile Selassie was their God!'

'I said be quiet. I don't care who their God is or where he is, he's not my God. I don't know what they think they are teaching at that school, but the Principal's going to hear from me.'

'But there's nothing wrong with Rastas or reggae music. Have you ever listened to it?' My sister and brother didn't even come to my rescue, and both of them listened to reggae music. 'Jonathon,' I said, 'tell Dad how much you like Peter Tosh.' Liking Peter Tosh meant, in my books, that there was still hope for Rib Roast: 'Go on tell him, he's not going to kill you, you know.' My brother didn't say a word, the yellow-bellied coward. Peter Tosh, Bob Marley, none of those people had had any effect on him. He just sat there looking down at his plate.

I turned to Jo-Ann. 'Jo, you borrowed all Ti-cush's reggae albums from me, didn't you? You think it's great music don't you?' She just rolled her eyes, maybe she was still angry with me about her fifty pounds. I hoped it all fell on her and crushed her – swine. Nobody helped, not even my mother who comes from Jamaica and knows differently.

'Tina, do you see what I mean? Do you see now what I have been telling you . . . ?'

'Never mind Dad, I'm not going to do the project. I don't want you going to the school – you're just going to embarrass me.'

'Embarrass you! Is that what you think of our interest in what you're learning? You children don't realise how important it is for Coloured People . . .'

'Here we go again: how important it is for Coloured People – underlined three times in red . . .' I clapped my hand over my mouth to shut myself up. I couldn't believe I had actually said what I had just said – but I had – I had said those words. My father was looking at me with his mouth open, then he shut it suddenly, as if he hadn't known he had had it open. I heard his teeth click as he closed his mouth and his eyes got sort of poppy – his face got darker and darker. *Everyone* was dead, dead quiet. I mean nobody, but nobody ever interrupts my father when he's talking – let alone to be rude like I had been.

Then he started again: 'All right, all right young woman' (young woman is worse than young lady), 'you are making it clearer and clearer to me that I have to take certain measures with you.' I looked at him. I knew what was coming. 'Tina we're going to write to my mother . . .'

'Cuthbert, go easy on her . . .' I couldn't believe my ears – my mother was actually saying something to defend me. 'You know how faysty she is . . .'

'She's too rude Tina, too rude. You're not doing your job properly. That's why I don't want you working . . .'

'Cuthbert . . .' was all my mother said, but her tone was real heavy.

The way my father huffed and puffed, I swear I could see puffs of smoke coming out of his ears. Then he said: 'I'm warning her, Tina, if there is one more incident like this, she's

41

going to my mother when school's out. Do you hear that young lady?' (I had moved back up to young lady.)

I was feeling real bad, it's so awful to have that sort of threat hanging over you. I mean it's bad enough that you don't get along with your family, but to be always worried about being sent away . . .

My mum must have felt sorry for me – she let me off the dishes that night. I went up to my room and lay across my bed for a while and cried. Zulma was coming over to spend the night but I couldn't even get excited about that. When she came, I told her what had happened.

'Maybe I'll run away with you Zulma.'

'Where we going to go though?'

'I don't know. I wish Harriet Tubman was around. She would help, she would know what to do, I know she would.'

Zulma was in the top bunk, I was below. She always liked to sleep there when she slept over; it made her feel like she was in her favourite mango tree back home. We had been talking like this for a while, then I said to her: 'Hey Zulma, would you call me Harriet? I would really like you to . . . Zulma? Zulma?'

There was no answer, Zulma had gone to sleep. I rolled over and repeated the name to myself: 'Harriet, Harriet, Harriet . . .' until I fell asleep.

8

Between worrying about getting Zulma home to her gran;
thinking of changing my name to Harriet; how to make the
changes in my life; and about being sent to Barbados if I
screwed up again, winter seemed to pass real quickly into
spring. Nothing had changed, but I was feeling more hopeful –
maybe it was a feeling of change in the air.

I had a plan I thought could help both my mother and
Zulma. I didn't know if my mother would go along with it, but
it was worth a try.

The first chance I saw my mother in the kitchen alone,
ironing, I grabbed it.

'Hey Mum – you want to work don't you?'

'Uh huh, but I can't find anything part-time right now, and
your dad don't want me working full-time.' What I muttered
under my breath was not very nice.

'What's that?' The radio was on, so my mum didn't hear, or
pretended not to hear.

'Oh nothing, but they're looking for teachers' aides at school
– four half days a week . . . so? What d'you think?'

'Uh huh.' My mother can play real dumb sometimes.

'Are you interested, Mum? I could give your name in at the
office.' There was a long pause before she answered.

'How come you want me in the same school with you?' She
was looking me straight in the eye. She was quick, my mother,
and sometimes she was dead on – like she was now. I really
didn't want her at the same school, but I had another plan.

'Oh I just thought it might get Dad off my back. You know how he goes on about e-du-ca-shun and Coloured People.'

'Don't be rude.'

'No Mum, really, if you're working there maybe he won't carry on so much.'

'Well, you can put in my name, but I don't want to be in your class – right?'

'Right.'

A week later my mum was called for an interview and she got the job. I let about a week go by after my mum started working, before I put the second part of my plan in action. My mum was in the kitchen alone: 'So how is the new job, Mum?'

'Fine.' She was ironing some shirts for my father – as usual.

'D'you like it?'

'Uh huh.' My mum was playing dumb again, but she was looking at me straight in the eye. She knew something was up, but I didn't blink or miss a beat.

'And Dad's happy – you're happy.' She looked hard at me again, but I went right on. 'And I'm happy . . . well not really happy, I can't do my reggae project; but everyone's happy, even Jo-Ann. She's got a new dress, and Rib Roast – well he's too dead to be happy . . .'

'Margaret! Stop it! What's going on?'

'Well, see . . . I was thinking . . .' Now it was my turn to pause, then I came out with it: 'Got paid yet?'

My mum gave me this real sharp look, real quick, then she looked down again at the shirt she was ironing. 'No, next week. Why?'

'You're glad I got you that job, right? Well, see – I was thinking that since I got you the job, maybe you could let me have half the money you make for Zulma's ticket – 'cause she's not happy.' My mother didn't say a word, she just kept on ironing.

'Did you hear what I said Mum?'

'I heard.'

'So?'

'So what?'

'What d'you think of the idea of giving me half the money you make? You know there are companies that find jobs for people, and they get paid for doing it – the companies I mean – I saw an article in the papers about it and . . .'

'And the answer is no, no, no, Margaret. Look at my mouth, N-O- spells no. I am not getting involved in what don't concern . . .'

'But Mum . . .'

'Don't "but Mum" me. I'm tired and I don't want to talk about it.' And she meant it; I could see that closed, shut-in look come over her face – like when she's tired of my father going on at her about something. So much for my plan to help her and Zulma. I was right where I was before with Zulma – no closer to getting her home.

I left my mum still ironing – didn't say goodnight or anything. Just reminded her that she was lucky I found her a job: 'You would have to pay a company hundreds of dollars for finding it for you. But I'm just a child right . . .' She didn't say anything. I went to my room to sulk – Jo-Ann wasn't even home for me to tease.

All this time, I was still thinking of changing my name; I had got Zulma and Ti-cush to start calling me Harriet. I had to work on my mum to see if she would agree to call me Harriet, but I didn't want to do it too soon after she refused to pay me my fee for finding her a job. Apart from being unfair, they were cheats as well.

It was about this time that I had another dream – a horrible one too: I was about six years old, wearing a long dress of some sort of dark blue cloth with tiny red flowers on it. I had a bonnet on my head, made out of the same cloth, and I was holding my mother's hand. I knew she was my mother, but she had Harriet Tubman's face; she was wearing a dress in the same cloth as mine, and a bonnet like mine. I had a long way to walk with her; I didn't know where we were going. As we walked, we passed through all these little towns and villages; each time we came to a town, my mother would begin to say to the people in the town: 'This is my daughter . . .' then she would stop as if she had forgotten my name. I was standing there, in the dream, feeling real foolish, then I would tug her hand and make her bend down; I would whisper in her ear, 'Harriet, Mum, Harriet.' My mother would just look at me, smile, shake her head and we would move on. I was getting more and more upset, in the dream, until finally I stopped whispering and started shouting, 'Harriet! Harriet! Harriet!' That woke me up with a start.

I was spending a lot of time thinking of Harriet Tubman and her life. I also thought about Harriet Blewchamp and how she managed to escape from a concentration camp – maybe she had a Harriet Tubman to help her. I made up secret codes that I, as Harriet, could pass to slaves who were trying to escape; with these codes, I could tell them when and where I was going to meet the slaves who wanted to run away. The codes were real simple. The brown cow needs milking meant that it wasn't safe for them and me to get together. The hens not laying today; the old hound dog tired, he not hunting tonight – all these meant danger, or delay. Jack rabbit running scared; mocking bird going call tonight; crescent moon and full moon never shine together – these meant we could meet and I would lead them to freedom. If I was caught, I knew I was as good as dead, but I *was* going to get those slaves to freedom if it killed me.

I used to dress up in my mum's long skirts and tie my head with her head-ties. It was when I was tying my head one day in my room that I got my chance to ask her about calling me Harriet. It was after school; she passed by my room and saw me struggling with the head-tie:

'Is what you think you doing?'

'Tying my head.'

'For what?'

'I'm pretending to be Harriet Tubman, that's what.'

'Who's Harriet Tubman?'

'A woman who brought slaves from the States to Canada – all by herself too.' By this time my mum was in my room sitting on a chair.

'Come here, let me tie that for you.' I went over to her and she tied my head real neat and nice.

'Gee Mum,' I said, looking in the mirror, 'that's real nice.'

'Hmmmmm.'

'Mum?'

'Yeeees . . .' she pulled out the yes like it was chewing gum. She knew I was going to ask her something she didn't want me to ask her. 'Is this about Zulma?'

'No, it's about me – my name. I want to change it – to Harriet.'

'Why?'

'Well, I like Harriet Tubman. I think she was real wonderful. I want a name that means something to me – Margaret doesn't mean anything to me at all. Also Mrs Blewchamp wanted me to have the name, Harriet.'

'Margaret is your grandmother's name; your father wanted you to have it.'

'I know that but it doesn't *mean* anything to me.'

'Why does your name have to mean something?'

'I don't know. Will you call me Harriet, will you? Say yes, pleeease Mum.'

My mother was quiet, real quiet, her face pulled in and closed.

'You mad with me or something, Mum?'

'No, just thinking.'

'About what?'

'My name.'

'*Your* name? Tina?'

'Tina is not my real name; Vashtina is my name and I hate it.' She sounded like she really hated it too.

'Vashtina? It's kind of ugly, Mum. Sounds like the name of a cow or something, but why d'you hate it?'

'When I was your age Margaret, that was all I used to hear,

47

"Vashtina do this, Vashtina do that, Vashtina come here, Vashtina go there." Sometimes I would have prefer die than hear my name call again.'

I sat on the bed and watched my mother; it was like she had forgotten I was there. She went on, 'When my mother die, I was just twelve. I had nowhere to go, no place to put my head, no bed, nothing. I used to sleep on some old bag, and most days it was one meal a day I was eating – red beans and rice – many a day, all I had for lunch was sugar water.

'I was living with my auntie then; she take me out of school and say that the only exam I was going pass was breeding. She send me to work with a family, and two months after I get there, the man in the house start brushing against me and want to come feel me up; so I run away from there, back home to my auntie. She beat me for running away; she didn't even want to listen to my story. So I run away again and went to a different cousin. She used to make me get up at five in the morning to milk the cow and goat – then I had to walk five miles to deliver milk. And every day a million time a day is "Vashtina": Vashtina fetch, Vashtina carry, Vashtina clean, Vashtina scrub and Vashtina wash – all day long. So no, I don't never want to hear the name Vashtina again. Even Tina too close to it, but to change it completely I have to go to a lawyer and go to court. Somehow I never seem ready to take that step.'

She was quiet after this. I was too. I don't know if she had ever talked about her name before; the way she talked made me think that she didn't talk about it much. Here I was thinking she had a cool name like Tina Turner and it was really Vashtina. I wondered what Tina Turner's real name was – probably something weird like Vashtina. I felt real sorry for my mum . . . I understood better why she always wanted to buy things for the house and for us . . . I wanted to cheer her up.

'Hey Mum,' I said, 'let's you and I change our names. I'll be Harriet, and you will be – what? I know, Hatshepsut, like Queen Hatshepsut of Egypt – she was a pharaoh. You're big and black and beautiful, just like her, and we'll call you Sut for

48

short.' She smiled, I was glad to see her smiling. 'So it's Hatshepsut, right?'

'Girl, you're real crazy, and you know your father not going to want to change your name.'

'But will *you* call me Harriet, Mum?'

She nodded. 'If you want.'

'Will you promise to talk to Dad about it?'

'To tell him what?'

'That I want to be called Harriet around the house.' My mum sighed, she was looking real old, and got up from the chair.

'Oh all right, but I wouldn't hold my breath.'

'Great.'

It was time for me to do a review of my THINGS I WANT CHANGED IN MY LIFE list. Number 1 – my father; number 3 – Zulma; number 4 – my sister; number 5 – my skin; and number 7 – my brother, were all unchanged. There was no way my brother was going to get even one pimple, so I took him off the list. Number 5 also came off – who was I kidding? There was no way I was going to get a blacker skin. In its place I put in more breasts with several question marks. I didn't want to ask for too much, then I'd have to wear Jo-Ann's bras, but a bit more I thought would be nice, so at least you could see something. Under number 5, I also added my period – I mean like *everyone* in my class, just about everyone had got theirs, except me. I was beginning to think I was a freak, or something.

There was no use talking to my mum about it; all she said was that it would happen when it happened, and that when it did, I mustn't let any boys touch me. 'Touch me Mum?' I said to her one day in the kitchen. She looked kind of embarrassed.

'Yes, touch you.'

'Where Mum, where mustn't they touch me?'

Jo-Ann was at the kitchen table when all this was going on; she was sniggering. My mother started slamming pots and pans around, and I asked her again.

'Where Mum?' She acted like she didn't hear me, and went

49

on slamming things around. I turned to Jo-Ann. 'Any boys touch you yet Jo?' And we both cracked up with laughter. My mum started smiling too, but she still didn't tell me where the boys were *not* to touch me. Hah, adults!

I took my mum off my list. She had a job; although she had finked out on paying my finder's fee, I think she was a lot happier.

Number 3 was a real loser though: Zulma, zilch. No go, negative – nothing, nothing, nothing. I had got twenty-one dollars and fourteen cents saved and that was it; yet I am rich, my mother's got four-thousand dollars of *my* money in the bank. Maybe I could hold up the bank, I thought, and take *my* money. I would have a slick, smooth, good-looking lawyer defend me – a woman of course – who would say: 'Your Honour, it was *her* money she was taking. How can she be stealing what belongs to her?' Ha! Ha! Fat chance. I would probably get a legal-aid lawyer who didn't give a damn about me. They would throw me in jail, throw away the key and I would never see Zulma again. I squashed what was a brilliant but stupid idea. But I was no further ahead with getting Zulma home.

I had made some changes in number 6 – my name: Zulma, Ti-cush and Mum were now calling me Harriet though I did notice that Mum didn't call me anything when HE was around. I was working on Jo-Ann, but she wanted me to pay her for calling me Harriet. I promised not to tease her, but she wanted ten dollars for a new Wham! album, or it's 'Margaret' for the rest of my life she says. Bugger her, I thought.

I made one more change to my list – excitement – I wanted excitement in my life. My life was Dullsville. If I couldn't help Zulma go back to her gran, and since I was living with the threat of being sent away for some GWID, I thought, I may as well have some excitement.

Right after adding excitement to my list, my mother called me to go and fetch my father. It was a Saturday evening and HE was off, yes, playing dominoes. This was not the kind of excitement I had in mind.

50

'Mum, why don't you call him? I'm busy.'

'He's at the Billings'; they always unplug the phone when they start playing dominoes. C'mon now Marg . . . I mean Harriet.'

'Oh, all right.'

9

I liked Mrs Billings. I called her Mrs B; it suited her. I didn't see her often, but whenever I did she was always happy and *always* had great food, homemade, which she was *always* offering me: cookies, cake, ice cream, cobbler, you name it Mrs B had it.

I'm sure she ate everything she made for she was really, really large but nice big, not big and slobby – big and . . . proud. She made big into a real nice word; if I had to be big I wanted to be big like Mrs B. She had big legs and a big bum, although she was much smaller on top – I mean her bosom. Her feet and hands were long and slim, almost like they didn't belong to the rest of her. She was tall too; 'five foot, eleven and three-quarter inches' she told me one day when I asked her; you could tell she was really proud of her height too. When she talked, her hands would flutter, like butterflies; Mrs B with the butterfly hands was how I thought of her.

Mrs B let me in when I got to her house. 'Hello Mrs B, is my dad here?'

'Hello Margaret. C'mon in child, c'mon in out of the cold. Yes, he's here, and so is everyone else including Mr Billings; have been ever since noon, and probably will be here this time tomorrow. How grown men can be so idle, I don't know. Go on down honey, you know where they are, in the basement. But before you leave come on up to the kitchen for some cookies. I just baked some, your favourite, chocolate chip.'

I had seen my dad play dominoes before, once or twice, maybe even more. I had forgotten how seriously they all took this stupid game. There they were – these big men – five, six, a lot of them just standing or sitting around the dominoes table. Some were drinking – not my dad though – he never drank and never let us forget The Evils of Alcohol. I mean this game wasn't even electronic. As I looked in the room they were playing in I saw this big, huge guy with a big stomach and little piggy eyes get up to make his play. He was holding a tiny little domino in one hand; I was just guessing this because the domino was so tiny and his hand was so big, you couldn't see anything. What I could see was him swinging his arm up and up above his head – then he slammed his hand down on the table – of course all the other pieces on the table jumped around like mad and he was yelling: 'Beat dat now, beat dat.'

'Hey that's cheating,' I said. Everyone including my father turned to look at me.

'What are you doing here?' he said. I could tell he was mad with me.

'Mum says dinner's ready.'

'Right, right, I'll be there. Go upstairs and wait for me.'

They were all concentrating on the game again. Adults! Dominoes! How stupid, I thought, and I meant both.

Upstairs in the kitchen, Mrs B had a package of cookies wrapped in grease-proof paper for me and some on a plate ready for me to eat, along with a glass of milk. 'C'mon child eat up. I can't eat them all myself.'

'Hmmm, oh thanks Mrs B.' My mouth was full of cookies and milk. 'Hmmm Mrs B – you're from the States, aren't you?'

'Uh huh.'

'Did you know anything about Harriet Tubman?'

She laughed. 'No,' then she giggled. It sounded almost like when me and Zulma giggle, but like music too and warm sounding. 'Well child, I may be pushing hard for sixty-five, but I never met her personally. Sure, I heard about Harriet Tubman. As a matter of fact she was supposed to have come from round about where I come from. Don't know much about her though. With all your studying, you probably know as much or more than I do. My family knew a few families whose

53

people came north with her, at least that's what the talk was, and that was a long time ago.'

'Really? Did any of your family come north with her?'

'Not as I know. I'm the first one who's come this far north . . . and I was escaping too . . .' She said the last very softly, almost like she didn't want to say it. Her face suddenly got serious, like my mum's does, and her hands stopped breaking the string beans. She was looking off into the distance like she had forgotten I was there; I didn't quite know what to say or do. Just then HE came up the stairs and came in the kitchen.

'Come on Margaret – Bertha – good to see you again.'

Mrs B shook herself and came back to the kitchen.

'Bye Cuthbert. Say hello to Tina for me. Tell her to come by and visit.'

'Bye Mrs B.'

'Bye Margaret. Come and give old Bertha a hug before you go.' Hugging Mrs B was like hugging a great big soft pillow. She held me close for a minute or so and I could smell her clean floury smell; then she held me away from her.

'Don't let an old lady's mumblings bother you child. Cheer up, and here are some more cookies.'

I still wasn't sure what had happened in the kitchen, but I smiled and followed HIM out to the car.

We sat in the car waiting for it to warm up, then I said: 'How come you play that game? Mum doesn't like it and gets upset when you play . . . besides, it seems kind of stupid.'

'I like it.' He eased the car into drive and moved it forward slowly.

'How come you don't let me do all the things I like then?'

'You're a child, I'm an adult, and I know what's best for you.'

'Why doesn't Mum like it anyway? I mean it's kind of stupid, but why does she get so upset when you play?'

My father was stopped at the red light and I could see him give me a quick look.

'It reminds her of things she wants to forget, I suppose.'

'Like her name?'

54

'How do you know about that?'

'Mum told me. How come you don't want to forget anything?'

He was real quiet, the car moved forward slowly.

'Dad?'

'What?'

'Don't you want to forget anything?'

'Don't ask so many questions, for heaven's sake!' I wasn't surprised; he always seemed angry with me – always – we could never talk, and he didn't like me, that was clear. Then he started, I should have known better than to get him started. He went on about how he and his friends used to make their own cricket bats from pieces of wood they found lying around; they used sticks for stumps. If there were no sticks they would use a piece of board, or even cardboard, and sometimes they would be even lucky enough to find a used cricket ball, its stitching half undone. 'Man those were the days: on the beach, in the hot sun, or during mango season when you would eat mangoes all day long and run to the bathroom all night long. All kinds of mango: green ones, yellow ones, red ones, long mangoes, starch mangoes, or mango calabash. Or we would shinny up a coconut tree faster than you could say Jack Robinson and pick coconuts – two or three cuts with the machete and you could have that nut to your head in no time flat. Stuck here in a city, you children today don't know what real childhood is all about, when the world is yours and you are the world.'

He looked at me as we pulled up in front of our house. 'Want to go live in Barbados for a while?'

'No. Why do you always keep on bugging me about that?'

I could tell I had hurt him and made him angry.

'Watch your mouth girl – that's Rudeness. Keep that up and you won't have a choice. You need some good Bajan training, that's what you need.'

10

I got a call from Zulma the following day. It was a Sunday; she was crying so hard I could hardly make out what she was saying. What I did get was that she wanted to come over and spend the night.

I yelled to my mum that I was going to Zulma's and was gone before she could check with my father; I wasn't grounded but you never knew.

I ran all the way to Zulma's house – as I got there she was coming out the front door. She was still crying but she was calmer than she was on the phone.

'What happened?'

She just shook her head and wiped her tears.

'C'mon let's hurry. Mum says I can stay up a bit and watch the James Bond movie on T.V. Maybe we can make some fudge and popcorn, eh?'

Zulma was smiling now. She loved James Bond movies; she had seen all the old ones in Tobago. She could even sing the *Goldfinger* song and boy! what a voice she had. The first time I heard her sing it, one evening after school in my room, I got goosebumps all over. When she opened her mouth this big sound came out – bigger than her and me; and it got rid of the shy, unhappy Zulma. All that was left was this voice that made me feel strong and, yes, even beautiful. I was dying for her to sing at the school concert, but she refused.

'Is what showing tonight?'

'*Thunderball.*'

'Oh great – me favourite.'

Later that night, after *Thunderball*, fudge and popcorn we were lying in the dark in my room, she in her tree house, me in a cave – stuck – that's how I felt.

'He hit me mother you know.'

'Who? Your stepfather?'

'Uh huh. Dey was having a fight 'bout money, or something – me was in me room doing me homework when me hear me mother crying – den plap, plap – two sounds like slaps, and me hear me mother cry out. Me run out to de living-room and me see he standing over she, and she a curl up on de couch like she fraid of he. But see me here, Margaret, me not fraid of he. He look 'pon me and say, "Go back to your room", and me say "Leave me mother alone." He a turn and begin to come towards me as if he want to hit me and I just a stand there. Marg – oh me mean Harriet, me was so frighten he going hit me – you see how big he is – and me know he hand could hurt; but me wasn't going budge, not one jot! Me gran always say, never let no man hit you, else he going want try it again and again. Me say to he: "Hit me, hit me, see if me don't call police for you." Me did remember dat class we did have 'bout child abuse, but Lord, me was frighten. When me mother hear what going on, she rush up from de couch and come and stand between we: "Please Lloyd, leave her alone. Please Lloyd." ' Zulma was taking off the way her mum spoke, real soft and gentle, then she sucked her teeth loudly.

'She so stupid. Imagine, he tell she dat she always trying to pick up for me and dat she won't let he discipline me – you hear dat Harriet, he want to discipline me – and dat no wonder me don't have no respect for he, and on and on like dat. Me ask me mother if me could go to your place and she say yes, so me run quick, quick and call you. You know me didn't cry all dat time when me was facing he, but just getting away from he make me realise how scared me was for me mother and meself. Me just start cry and cry, and dat's when me call you.' I thought she was going to cry again but she didn't.

'Harriet me hate he so much sometimes, you know . . . and she just can't see how terrible he is to she. She have to give he all she money every week, den he give she back some. He want to know everything she spend money on and she can't go nowhere without he. He don't like she spending too much time with me – he say she spoil me . . . why she stay with he, me don't know. If me gran only know what going on, she would find some way to come and take me back home, but me can't write and tell she – me fraid she get a stroke or something.'

I didn't say anything. I couldn't.

'You awake Harriet?'

'Uh huh – just thinking . . . you know it's too bad we can't get your stepfather deported. That would solve the problem . . . for you and your mother.'

'Deported? Is what dat?'

'I heard Mum and Dad talking about someone they knew who got deported back to the West Indies. It's when Immigration sends you back to where you came from.'

'Just so? You think maybe dey could deport me back?'

'I don't think so . . . I sort of got the feeling that you have to do something wrong, or be here without permission, something like that . . . but deportation would solve it, wouldn't it?'

'But he don't do nothing wrong – except hit me mother. You think dat wrong enough to get he deported?'

'I don't know . . . anyway, I think your mother would have to report him to the police.'

'No way! She never do that – she say she love he.'

'How can she love him if he hits her?'

'Me don't know – don't ask me. Dat's de way adults is – some adults – not me gran. She don't take nothing from nobody.'

'D'you think we'll get like that when we grow up?'

'Me? Never!'

'What are you going to do – about your stepfather?'

'Me going run away, far away.'

'You can't just run away – where would you stay? Who would look after you, and what about school? You can't run

away Zulma, you can't . . . at least not without me. If you run –
I run.'

I was getting more and more upset.

'Yes me can and me going do it.'

'You don't have any money. Where are you going to stay?
Can't you hold on for a while?' I was getting desperate – and
bolder.

'I'm trying to work something out with my mum about
buying a fare for you to go back to your gran.'

'Dat would be great. How come you never tell me 'bout dis?'

'Well, the money my mum has saved for me . . . I may be
able to get something from it but it takes time – you know with
forms to fill out and all that . . . ' I crossed my fingers and legs
and eyes, tightly, as tight as I could to wipe out the lies I was
telling. I was not working out anything with my mother; I had
no way or hope, short of a miracle, of getting money for Zulma's
fare. I was lying through my teeth, but I had to prevent Zulma
from running away before we had some sort of plan.

'You've got to be patient Zulma; it's going to take some time
because we have to – not me – but my mother has to talk to the
lawyer about it.' My lies were coming fast and more easily. I
was really only trying to make Zulma feel better.

'If I can't get the money for your fare Zulma, I'll run away
with you – I promise you.'

'With me? You can't do dat. How 'bout your parents? You
don't have no cause to run away.'

'Yes I do – as much as you – well, not as much, but almost as
much. My father is always threatening to send me away, and he
doesn't like me . . . at least not as much as Jo-Ann – his
"cinnamon girl" – and I'm not a boy like Jonathon, or not as
stupid, thank God.'

'Your mother like you though.'

'Yeah, sort of, but she's not really happy with me. I'm just not
what she wants me to be – like Jo-Ann. Her face is all smiles
when Jo-Ann goes to show her a new dress, or new make-up.
With me she's kind of uncomfortable. You're lucky you don't

59

have any brothers or sisters to be compared with . . . you're also lucky you have someone like your gran who believes in you . . . Nobody believes in me.'

We were silent – seemed like for a long time.

'Zulma? Zulma?'

There was only regular breathing from the bunk above. I couldn't fall asleep; I just lay there thinking of my promise to get Zulma back to Tobago, and my lies. I felt my nose – no it wasn't getting any bigger, but my heart was really heavy – felt like it weighed a lot. Zulma had been getting the hang of school, liking it more, she had even made a few friends in her class but she hadn't forgotten about Tobago, or about going back there to her gran. And I didn't know how the hell I was going to get her there with no money. My mother had gone and squashed all my plans to help her. I wondered if Harriet would have been able to help. I was sure she would have been able to. That night my dreams were all of Harriet Tubman – she was helping Zulma escape to Canada, and me to Tobago.

11

It was because my life was dull, dull, dull. It was because I wanted some excitement in my life. It was because I admired Harriet Tubman and wanted to change my name to Harriet. It was because, it was because; it was because nothing. It just happened – the game, the Underground Railroad Game.

We – Zulma, Ti-cush and I – were hanging out in my room one Saturday afternoon, dancing to reggae music; Zulma was braiding my hair in between sets. She didn't do as good a job as my mum, but when my mum got huffy with me, as she had been for the last week, Zulma did it. Ti-cush was in one of her 'Life sucks' moods and I was desperate, just plain old desperate over not being able to help Zulma.

Zulma put on a Wailers album and began to sing along with Bob Marley. The song was *No Woman, No Cry*, and as she sang the song became her song. Goosebumps came up again on my skin as her big voice painted pictures of Trench Town ghettoes and love. When she sang the refrain, 'no woman, no cry', it was like she was telling herself – her mum, her gran, maybe even me, not to cry – and all I could do was cry. I felt like a real suck as the tears rolled down my cheeks; I *never* cry, not even in movies, but I cried when Zulma sang, 'no woman, no cry'. But it wasn't just sucky, sentimental feelings, I also felt like fighting too; oh yes, that Zulma could sing.

When she was done everyone was quiet, real quiet.

'You guys don't like it?'

We still didn't say anything then I said: 'You've got to, you just have to sing it at the school concert, Zulma.'

61

'Nah man, dis is just for me friends.'

'You like it Ti-cush?'

Ti-cush didn't look up; she just nodded, got up quickly and said she had to go to the bathroom.

'You think she like it Marg . . . I mean Harriet?'

'I'm sure she did – I think she was crying – that's why she rushed off to the bathroom really.'

'You think so?'

'Yep. You should really sing it at the concert.'

'I going to think about it. Hey let me finish your hair.'

When Ti-cush came back – she looked like she had had a really good cry – she started messing around in my drawers.

'Hey Harriet, don't you have any lipstick?'

'Uh uh – check with Jo-Ann – she's got enough for us all.'

Ti-cush left and came back with three different shades of lipstick and two shades of eye make-up.

'Look what I got guys,' she showed us her haul. 'Boy does she ever have lots of make-up.' She stood close to the mirror and began to make up her face.

'Listen up guys,' I said, 'I want to talk to you about something.'

'Uh huh,' said Ti-cush. She leant even closer to the mirror and pouted her 'Luscious Cherry' lips; she was tightening and rolling her lips together to spread the lipstick, like I had seen my mum and Jo-Ann do a million times. 'You got any Kleenex, Harriet? I've got to blot my lips.'

'Look in the bathroom. Are you guys listening? I was thinking of playing a game.'

'Game? What kind of game?' This was Ti-cush; she was busy spreading Tropical Purple blusher on her cheeks and she looked awful.

'Ti-cush, this is serious – are you interested in this or in make-up?'

'I'm listening – I can do this and listen you know.' She was rolling her lips together again, but this time with a sheet of

Kleenex stuck between them; she looked like some paper-eating monster. 'What kind of game is it? You never answered.'

'An Underground Railroad Game.'

'Underground Railroad Game?'

'Stop repeating everything I say Ti-cush.'

'Well I don't know what you're talking about.' Now she was tackling her eyes with the Frosted Bronze Girl eye-shadow.

I pulled away from Zulma who was still combing my hair: 'Look guys, just pay attention for a while.'

Ti-cush started giggling.

'What are you laughing at?' I asked her.

'You – you look funny – look in the mirror.' I looked: one half of my hair was braided in neat and tight, the other half stood up straight. I looked like a half-surprised rabbit.

'So? I look funny. But you do too, with your awful make-up. Come on guys listen up – please.

'I was thinking we could set up a kind of Underground Railroad right here, with other kids, you know: choose slaves, slave-owners, dogs, guides, safe houses, and have a game with slave-owners and dogs trying to find the slaves. We could have a place that would be "Freedom", and the slaves would have to try to get from slavery to "Freedom" . . . well? What d'you guys think?'

'Dogs? Real dogs?' Ti-cush had stopped putting on her make-up and stared at me in the mirror. She looked like a real freak – one eye with some frosted bronze goop, the other normal – but I could tell she was interested.

'No, Ti-cush,' I said, making it plain that I thought her question was stupid, 'not real dogs.'

'You know,' Ti-cush said, 'I heard that a lot of those slave-owners had mistresses, beautiful mistresses. I could be someone's mistress.'

'Do you know what a mistress is?' I asked her.

'Well . . . not really, but it sounded like fun.'

I started to laugh. 'Ti-cush, you're impossible. I wasn't planning on having mistresses, but what d'you think Zulma?'

63

Zulma was still holding the comb in her hand. I had forgotten all about my hair.

'It sound like fun, don't it Ti-cush? Let we try it, nuh?'

'Sure, let me finish this other eye.' She covered her other eye with the bronze mess and came over to where I was sitting on the floor. 'This all has to do with your being Harriet Tubman, eh?'

'Sort of, c'mon sit down and help. Pass me that pencil over there.'

'Are we only going to have black slaves?' That was Ti-cush's question. I looked at her; I was surprised, I hadn't thought of this. I mean I thought that all slaves were black, but Ti-cush's question made me think. I was biting hard on my pencil, so hard I broke it.

'Can slaves be white?' I asked this out loud, to myself more than to either Zulma or Ti-cush. They were watching me and not saying anything. Could slaves be white, could they? I asked myself. Why not? I had answered my own question. 'Hell anybody can be a slave, right? It just so happened that black people were for a while – I mean slaves – right? You guys agree?'

They both nodded, and I wrote in big block letters: RULES FOR THE UNDERGROUND RAILROAD GAME: (1) Anyone can be a slave.

'Oh! I forgot one of the most important rules: the game must be kept a secret – right guys? We must have that rule. If you break it you're out of the game for good.' *That will probably be the end of the game too*, I muttered to myself under my breath as I wrote: (2) Game must be a secret. 'o.k. Zulma, how about you being in charge of the safe houses . . . ? and Ti-cush you could be in charge of the slave-owners and dogs. I'll be in charge of the guides and slaves.'

'Hey wait up Margaret, what is a safe house?'

'I don't want to be in charge of slave-owners or dogs.'

Ti-cush and Zulma had both spoken together; they looked at each other and began laughing.

'O.K. O.K., let me explain. When slaves were running away, they used to travel by night – not all the time but most of the time – and hide during the day, because the slave-owners would send people to look for them. Not all white people liked slavery, or wanted slaves; some of them even began to help slaves escape by hiding them in their houses, or giving them food and clothes – sometimes they even disguised them. Safe houses were those houses where slaves could go and be safe while they were running away.'

'Kind of like hide-and-seek when you get home.'

'Sort of like that, except "home" really would be freedom and Canada. Safe houses were like in-between "homes" – little "homes".'

'I don't want to be in charge of slave-owners or dogs. I want to do something else. I'm sure no one is going to want to be a dog or a slave-owner . . . isn't there something more . . . glamorous?'

'Well someone has to be in charge of them; I think you'd be better at it than Zulma.' Ti-cush's face came over all heavy and sullen and stubborn – like a mule I suppose except I had never seen one – a mule I mean. 'Oh come on Ti-cush – you'll see, you'll get lots of people for dogs and slave-owners and it's only a game – you don't have to take it so seriously.'

'Where slavery going to be?' Zulma asked.

'Take a guess.'

'School?'

'Right on – the school yard. "Freedom" has to be a secret though – only the guides and slaves are going to know.'

'Why?' asked Ti-cush, 'why can't I know?'

'Ti-cush if you know, there's no point to the game. All you'd have to do is come to "Freedom" and wait there for the slaves and guides. The whole point of the game is that "Freedom" is a secret, and . . .'

'In real life it wasn't,' she said, 'everyone knew they were going to Canada, even . . .'

'But the slave-owners didn't know *exactly* where the slaves

65

were going to enter Canada – there were hundreds of routes. Look Ti-cush, we can't have the game without you – we need the slave-owners and dogs as much as we need the slaves, and we need *you*.' Her face got softer – a teensy weensy bit softer – and her Luscious Cherry mouth wasn't so pouty.

'Oh all right; but I bet you no one wants to be a dog or a slave-owner.'

'Maybe – we'll see. Can we check that we've got everything; let's see, we've got slaves, slave-owners, dogs, safe houses, "Freedom", oh, maps. We need maps because we're going to have several different routes to "Freedom", just like in the old days. You know what guys, we should walk around all the streets in this area and draw our maps.'

'How it going work though Harriet?' Zulma asked.

'Easy: look, let's say we have ten ways of getting to "Freedom" from slavery. Every Saturday we'll choose say three routes, and every one will start from the school yard – slavery. The slaves and guides are going to have some lead time on the slave-owners and dogs. Slave-owners and dogs will also know the routes, but the slave-owners won't know which of those three routes the slaves will use. Now, we have got to stick to those three routes, but we can switch between them – and all the routes will end at St Clair, but not at "Freedom" right? It will be up to the slave-owners and dogs to find us . . .'

'Before you get to "Freedom" right?' Ti-cush was interested again.

'Right.'

'But how are you going to stop us seeing you leave slavery – I mean the school yard?'

That one had us stumped for a while. After a lot of talk we finally agreed that the slave-owners and dogs would all gather at Ti-cush's home. She lived about five minutes' walk from the school. We – the slaves and guides – would call her from the phone booth just outside the school playground and tell her when we were leaving; the slave-owners and dogs would then leave and come to the school to start tracking us. Just after our phone call, and before we 'escaped' we – the slaves and guides – would have to count to one hundred. This was so that we wouldn't have too big a lead on them.

We agreed to meet Monday, in the playground, at recess time. 'Talk to your friends Ti-cush,' I said, 'and bring them with you. We'll meet over by the baseball diamond.'

Ti-cush stuck a piece of gum in her mouth and began chewing it: 'Uh huh – O.K. You guys want some gum?'

'Hate the stuff,' I said. Zulma took some.

'Look,' Ti-cush said, 'I gotta go now – got a job to do for my mother.' She was cracking her gum.

'Come out with us tomorrow to make the maps,' I said to her.

She cracked her gum some more: 'Can't, promised my mum to do something for her. See you guys.'

'Hey, Ti-cush,' I called out, 'remember to keep it a secret, O.K.?' She nodded and stalked off.

12

I wish there was someone there to video me. I did Harriet proud, real proud the day I talked to the kids. I had tied my head in the washroom before I met them. No way could I have done it at home; my mother was sure to tell me she wasn't dead yet. So there I was facing all those kids. I told them what the game was all about: explained about safe houses, guides, and so on – and they were with me all the way. By the time I had finished, recess was over, but we were going to meet right after school. As we went back into school, I could hear them talking about who was going to be a slave, or a dog or a slave-owner, and why it was better to be a slave rather than a slave-owner or dog. I heard one kid say, 'Well, we can't all be slaves'; and another one that dogs were 'better than slave-owners because they didn't have minds of their own'.

They were still with me when we met again after school, until it came time to volunteer as dogs or slave-owners. Ti-cush was right. Nobody, but nobody, wanted to be either.

'See, I told you so.' Ti-cush sounded real pleased and vicious about being right. I tried my best to persuade them, explaining how much the game needed them, 'as much as we need slaves'. No dice. Nobody volunteered – only a low mutter from them.

I pleaded: 'It's just a game. You're not really a slave-owner.' Nothing. I tried bribery: 'How about if we say the slave-owners and dogs don't have to pay, and they get treated every Saturday at McDonald's?' (We had agreed that everyone would contribute fifty cents a week to buy treats for the slaves who got to 'Freedom'.) That still didn't grab them. Ti-cush was muttering under her breath about how she'd known no one would want to be a slave-owner or dog.

Then she spoke up, 'I think this game really sucks,' and curled her top lip like only Ti-cush could. I had often wished I could curl my lip like that, and even practised it but gave it up as a lost cause. She wasn't finished either. 'Who wants to go running around dressed up like slaves and dogs? That's just for little kids – right guys?' She looked around her for support which she got.

Some kids nodded; I heard someone say, 'Yeah, it sucks,' and one or two others muttered, 'That's right, this is for kids.'

'Ti-cush is right – I consider it much too juvenile for me.' I recognised Chrissie Campbell's voice – she was always trying to impress and show off. Kids would often mock the way she spoke, and right to her face too, but she never seemed to notice it. When we wanted to shut her up we used to call her Lake Superior. That day I wanted to tell her to shut up, get lost, and drop dead – all at once, but I knew I had greater trouble than Chrissie Campbell, so instead I yelled, 'Hey, wait up guys! Ever heard about Dungeons and Dragons – D&D?'

That got their attention. Chrissie Campbell was nodding vigorously to show that she knew about the game. I was surprised she didn't say she had one.

'Well, don't all kinds of people play that game – kids who are much older than us – even adults, right?'

'Hey, that's true guys.'

I don't remember who said that, but I knew I had them, so I continued, 'And just last week I read something in the papers about university students playing war games – they dressed up like soldiers and were using guns.'

'Yeah, and someone got hurt,' Darren McAllister said. 'He lost his eye. My dad was telling me about it: the guns weren't real guns, but they could still hurt you.'

'Look,' I said, 'if you don't want to dress up you don't have to, but we can still play the game – with or without dressing up.'

Everyone was nodding now. I took a deep breath and let it out slowly. That Ti-cush had almost gone and wrecked the game even before it got started, and boy was I glad I had remembered about Dungeons and Dragons and war games – was I glad.

'So guys, who's going to volunteer?' I looked around but there were still no hands.

Suddenly – I think it was David Shaw who said it – I always thought he was a little creep, but was I grateful to him that day: 'Why don't we draw names from a hat; that way no one has to volunteer to be someone they don't want to be, they would be chosen.' I could have kissed him – yikes! Everyone was nodding and smiling and agreeing now, so I wrote their names on a piece of paper and tore them into little pieces. Zulma folded them, someone lent their toque, and Ti-cush, looking real mean and ugly, got to pick eight names for slave-owners and dogs. Zulma then picked eight slaves and I picked four guides.

Pina Francesconi had been picked as a slave, but she said she had to babysit her little brother Sandro on Saturdays. She wanted to bring him with her but he was only seven years old. I thought he was too little, but another girl, Maria I think it was, said she wasn't going to play unless Pina could play. Someone else added that slaves used to take their children with them when they ran away – so we all agreed that Pina's brother would be the youngest of ten slaves (including Zulma). Pina promised she would make sure he didn't breathe a word to anyone; she would bribe him, if she had to.

We hung about and talked some more about the game, but already the group began to split up. The slaves and guides stood close to me and Zulma; the slave-owners and dogs stuck close to Ti-cush, who looked like she wanted to fire them all.

All that week our group of slaves and guides met and talked – we chose our safe houses and made up stories to tell our parents, if they asked questions about why so many of us were visiting all at once: we were doing group projects. We chose our routes: three routes to 'Freedom' – the old deserted YMCA building at the corner of St Clair and Robina – I had found a way in through a broken window.

As I said before, some people might say that the game began it all – my problems, that is. Others might say it all began with my parents but as I said before, everything began with them so that wasn't really saying anything. Maybe the game was my way of pretending to escape with Zulma from all our problems; maybe it was my way of putting some excitement in my life – and it did put some excitement in my life; maybe it was all those things.

The first time we played, we hid behind a hedge, got chased by a humungous German Shepherd dog and yelled at by its owner, but we made it to 'Freedom', my group and Zulma's. We waited for the other group, but they didn't show up, so we went to the McDonald's on St Clair. We had agreed to meet everyone there. We did.

The other slaves *had* got caught: they had hung around the school yard to spy on the slave-owners and dogs. They wanted to see what direction the owners and dogs would take – their plan was to take the opposite direction. It would have worked, Gino Fratecelli said, except that some of the slave-owners and dogs had doubled back and caught them. 'Why did you guys come back anyway?' he asked.

'To see if there were any other clues stupid, and . . .'

'That's not fair, we didn't even have a chance to leave the school yard. There were these guys howling like dogs, and the slave-owners yelling, "Stop dead! Stop dead!" ' This was how Ti-cush and her group were going to let us know if and when they spotted us. One group was real happy, another group was looking real down.

'C'mon guys,' I said, 'cheer up. We've got next week, but remember – if you get caught again, you miss a week, so try and not get caught, O.K.' I turned to Ti-cush, 'So how was it?'

71

'o.k.' She still didn't look happy, and I couldn't figure it out. It was her group that had caught the slaves, yet she wasn't happy. But then that was Ti-cush: 'Life sucks', was her motto, and that was how she looked that day – like life sucked.

13

We played the game for about six more weeks. Some weeks
nothing much happened, but we did have some exciting times,
and it helped Zulma forget her problems (that's what I was
hoping for at least). It took my mind off my promise to help her,
and my failure *and* I was having some excitement.

Everyone who played the game called me Harriet, and that
was just great – my mum too, and Jo-Ann sometimes, but if she
really wanted to bug me she would 'Margaret' me to death in
one sentence. She would start off a sentence: 'Margaret,
Margaret, Margaret, Mum wants you, Margaret, to go downstairs, Margaret, and get the laundry, Margaret, in the
basement, Margaret.' I could still shut her up with Slobbo, or
Chub Queen, or Cinnamon Roly Poly. I promised not to tease
her if she would call me Harriet – half a week was all we could
manage.

HE absolutely refused to call me Harriet; my mother was
right, said it would only give me ideas, which were bound to get
me in trouble.

But the game – when we were on, we were really on. One
week we decided to dress up like real slaves and dogs and slave-
owners. Some of the slaves wore cut-offs; we – the girls –
decided to tie our heads and wear long skirts. We were all
joking about how people would think we were weird and
wonder what we were doing dressing up like Hallowe'en so
early in the year. We didn't care though – we were so into the
game by then – all that mattered was playing it. I wanted to

lead the *whole* group like Harriet did, we were not going to split up.

We had left a few false clues along two of the trails: I had sprinkled some flour on the sidewalk; we had tied some pieces of ribbon in some hedges – marked a few poles with chalk – then we set off.

About five minutes into our escape, we heard the dogs and owners – the dogs were barking, the owners shouting. I was sure I could hear a real dog, not just the kids pretending to be dogs. We didn't know what to do; there were no safe houses on the street, no hedges, then I saw the cars. 'Quick,' I said, 'the cars!' We quickly tried the doors on a few cars; some were open so we piled into them and crouched down low. It was a tight squeeze in my car, but we heard them, the dogs and owners, go by without spotting any of us. Once they passed, I lifted my head to look – oh hell, there *was* a real dog. Who had brought a dog?

We still had a way to go, so we got out of the cars and made a dash up a lane on to another street. Zulma went ahead to check the next two cross streets. She came back, yes, another group of owners and dogs were coming up the second cross street; unless we turned back we were bound to meet them.

'All right guys,' I said, 'there are two safe houses on this street – let's split up for now until they pass – then we'll come together again. Zulma, you take Franca's house, I'll take Rosa's.'

That was a mistake: Rosa was in Zulma's group, Franca in mine. When my group got to Rosa's house, we found that it wasn't a very safe house. No, we couldn't come in, Rosa's mother told us, because Rosa wasn't there. We told her that Rosa said we could come in and wait for her – yes, we could wait for her but on the porch.

The door closed on us then just as quickly opened again and Rosa's mother's face appeared at the glassed-in screen door.

'Why are you kids dressed like that?' Before we could make up an answer, she went on, 'You'll catch your death of cold in

74

this weather. Look at you,' she pointed at someone in cut-offs. 'I bet your mother doesn't know you're out dressed like that.' The fact that some of us were in long skirts and wore head-ties didn't seem to bother her at all – I suppose because we looked more warmly dressed. I'll never understand adults. 'Go on home and dress warmly,' she said and closed the inner door behind her, and not a second too soon, for we could hear the slave-owners coming. No sooner had Rosa's mother closed the door than we threw ourselves on to the floor of the porch – not a bloody second too soon – and lucky there was no fancy iron grill-work on this porch. It was a wooden porch with solid wooden sides.

Meantime, Zulma's group, as we found out later, was having the same problem at Franca's house. Franca's parents wouldn't let them in; worse luck, their porch *did* have fancy iron grill-work. They had to run around the back of the house to hide.

Pina's brother was in our group and he was in tears by this time. He had heard the dog barking, and he was sure it was the German Shepherd dog coming to get him. When we came together again, Pina, who was in Zulma's group, had to bribe him with some more of her pocket money to keep him quiet. Pina was spending just about all her pocket money buying gum to keep him quiet.

We were two streets away from 'Freedom' now, so we went through several backyards until we came to the big parking lot just below the YMCA building. We climbed up the steep bank and hauled ourselves through the broken window. We were there again! Freedom!

When we got to the McDonald's that day, Ti-cush was really angry they hadn't caught anyone. I refused to let it get me down though. Everyone was dressed up – some of the slave-owners were wearing red lumberjack jackets and hats; some had painted on moustaches; and some kids had made dog masks.

'So how come you guys are all dressed like men?' I asked.

'Cause we're slave-owners.'

'So?' I said. 'There were women slave-owners too, you know, *and* they hunted runaway slaves.' They laughed.

75

'Aw come on Harriet, most of them were men right?' I couldn't say no to that.

'And who brought the dog?'

'It was Frankie – he said it never barked.'

'Dat dog bark more than any other dog me ever hear,' said Zulma.

'And it scared Sandro a lot too.' Pina was mad about having to pay out more of her pocket money.

'He only barks when he's excited . . .' Frankie was trying hard to apologise for his dog, '. . . I didn't think he would bark so much.'

'You said you wanted us to dress up like real slave-owners – so what's wrong with a real dog?' That was life-sucks-Ti-cush.

'I didn't say anything was wrong Ti-cush. What's wrong with you anyway?'

'Nothing.' She got up and left – life still sucked for her, obviously.

Then there was the time I had the idea to make the game more exciting. I got the group, our group, together at the baseball diamond, and explained what we had to do.

'Jeez,' someone said, 'they'll never catch us now.'

'Boy, they're going to be mad.'

'Well let's see what happens,' I said.

That Saturday we met at 'slavery' as usual. I held some papers in my hand; on them I had written the words FREE PAPERS. I gave these to four of the slaves. 'O.K., you guys are decoys – right. Let the owners and dogs find you, but don't make it look too easy. Run away and sort of hide, but not so that they can't find you. Then when they catch you – present your FREE PAPERS – they have to let you go. That way the others will have a chance to get to "Freedom".'

I wasn't there, but I heard that Ti-cush and a group of slave-owners and dogs saw Franca; they yelled, 'Stop dead! Stop dead!' Franca stopped, and when they came up to her, she flashed her FREE PAPERS at them.

'I'm free,' she said, 'free – you can't catch me.'

Ti-cush grabbed the papers: 'What's this crap?'

'They're my FREE PAPERS – read it – it says I'm free. Harriet says we're free.'

'Harriet! Harriet! Harriet!' Ti-cush yelled, 'I'm sick of Harriet, and this lousy game.' She then spat on the sidewalk and walked off.

I heard all this at McDonald's. Some of the slave-owners and dogs felt I should have told them before – that that was why Ti-cush was so angry.

'Ti-cush is *always* angry, and we don't have to tell you guys everything,' I said. 'The real slaves didn't tell the owners what they were going to do so they could escape. If we had told you, it wouldn't have been a surprise – we couldn't have escaped.'

'Well Ti-cush is pretty mad. I don't think she's going to play again.'

'I'll talk to her,' I said.

We went to Ti-cush's house later on that day – Zulma and me. Ti-cush came out on the porch to talk to us.

'So what's up?' I asked. 'I heard you were mad with me.'

'You, that's what's up, you! How come you go and change the rules and don't tell me? Who d'you think you are anyway, with your new name and your stupid game?'

'O.K., O.K.,' I said. 'I'm sorry for not telling you, but I didn't think I was changing the rules. I thought it would be fun, that's all.'

'Well it wasn't.'

'The others liked it.'

'That's cause they're all sucks.'

'O.K., O.K., are you still playing?'

'Maybe.'

'I've got to know – now.'

'Oh all right then.' Her face was sullen and she wouldn't meet my eyes.

'I'm not leading a group next week,' I said. 'I'm going straight to "Freedom" with Pina's brother. He's getting really scared and having all kinds of nightmares, so I'm going to babysit him this week. We are all going to take turns doing it.'

Ti-cush didn't say anything; we just stood around for a while not saying anything to each other, we didn't quite know what else to do or say.

'Look, I gotta go and do something for my mother,' Ti-cush broke the silence. We were relieved to leave.

'Me don't trust she at all Margaret. Me blood just don't take to she.'

'Oh come on, Zulma, she's just upset. You know how Ti-cush gets.'

Zulma shrugged and didn't say anything else.

The following Saturday, the slaves split up into two groups, with one guide each. Zulma had decided to babysit with me at 'Freedom'. The decoys were so much fun, the others were going to use them again.

We tried to entertain Sandro as best we could; we read him stories, played hide-and-go-seek, and when we ran out of things to do, gave him piggy-back rides. By one o'clock, no one had yet shown up. Sandro was really bored and wanted to go outside; he began to whine and ask for his sister. We were getting more and more anxious.

'It's funny no one's come yet,' I said to Zulma.

'Maybe de dogs catch dem.'

'All of them? Let's go outside and see if we can spot anyone.'

There was no one outside the YMCA, so we walked toward the school. Before we got to the school, we could hear the ruckus – something was going on. The yelling and shouting got louder and louder as we got closer.

'What's going on?' I asked one of the kids.

'Someone finked, that's what is going on,' one boy said to me. 'I think it's her,' he said, pointing to Ti-cush. He spat.

'You come here and tell me that.' Ti-cush was spoiling for a fight, her hands curled into tight, hard fists. 'I'll show you who the fink is.'

'Pina what happened?'

'We all got caught. We were in two separate groups, but one after another we got caught – and real close to "Freedom" too. It's funny but there weren't any slave-owners or dogs along the routes. I think they know where "Freedom" is.'

'No we don't.' This from one of the owners, but they looked guilty as hell to me. Some of them wouldn't meet my eyes. The slaves and guides were still mad with them, and the groups were still exchanging insults.

I figured that even if they didn't know where "Freedom" was, they knew the general location; all they had to do was hang around there, and they were bound to pick us up – slaves and guides.

'o.к., look guys,' I said, 'there's no point fighting about it. D'you still want to play?'

They did. 'Well we've got to change the location of "Freedom",' I said. 'Since we're doing that, why don't we switch? Slaves can be owners, or dogs, and owners and dogs can be slaves. What d'you think?'

Nobody wanted to change – they were happy with their roles – all except life-sucks-Ti-cush.

14

After we changed 'Freedom', the game was less and less fun. We did have one more really exciting time, when we played at night. It was actually a lot more fun looking back on it than it was at the time.

We waited until our parents were asleep; at two o'clock in the morning we met at 'slavery' and set off. We were all nervous, but it felt a lot more like how it must have been with Harriet Tubman. Some of us didn't make it that night, only my group did and it was pure luck that we did, but everyone thought it was worth it – even Ti-cush.

We had been stooping low, walking close to hedges, going through people's backyards, then someone said a real bad word: 'Cops!' Jeez, I thought, if we got caught, the cops were bound to call our parents – in my case that would be certain death. Just thinking of cops calling my father at 3 o'clock in the morning to tell him they had his daughter . . . my mind went blank, I was so scared I stopped breathing, then I noticed my underarms were pouring sweat. This always happened when I was nervous or scared.

We all lay on the ground behind the hedge and held our breaths. I could hear a dog growling in the yard, I prayed it wouldn't start barking or come for us. Thank God Sandro wasn't with us; it would have been game over.

The cruiser went by, I let out my breath slowly and when we could no longer see its tail lights, we ran hard for 'Freedom', not caring whether or not we were caught. The other slaves had the same problem, I found out later, except that they saw the cops after the slave-owners and dogs had caught them. Everyone – slaves, guides, slave-owners and dogs – had to hide from the police. It was a strange feeling, they said, to feel that they were all on the same side, hiding from the cops.

When we got to 'Freedom', I was beginning to regret suggesting that we play the game late at night. I took a real deep breath before going into the blackness of our new 'Freedom' (it was an old, deserted church just south of St Clair Avenue). I could tell that we were all scared, but we were all acting real cool. We were there for about ten minutes; it seemed like a lifetime, in the blackness, but we didn't want to hang around any longer for the others. We were just about to crawl through the basement window, which hadn't been shut properly, when we heard a voice outside and saw a light like a flashlight. We all ducked down; I was so scared I thought I would pee myself. Then we heard someone trying the door to the basement, and whoever it was – probably the cops – shone a light through several of the basement windows. My heart was going – I don't know what a sledge-hammer sounds like, but I'm sure it sounds like my heart sounded that night. My mouth was dry. Then it got quiet again and I thought I heard a car drive away. Nobody moved for a long time, a really long time, then my legs began to get pins and needles, so I had to move.

Quickly and quietly, we climbed through the window and went home. I let myself in quietly and went up to my room, and would you know it, my dear sister was up – waiting for me.

'I'm going to tell on you. Where have you been? You've been meeting some boy haven't you?'

'No stupid, I leave that to you,' I whispered back.

'I'm going to tell Dad on you unless . . .'

'Unless what, Fatso?' She wanted me to beg her, but I wouldn't, I wouldn't.

'You tell Dad on me and I'll tell him I saw you necking with your pimply-face boyfriend on the porch.'

'You never did!'

'I know that, but Dad doesn't, and you know how he gets

81

about you and boys. I'll also tell him you meet him at McDonald's – and you *know* that's true.'

Jo-Ann had another three months to go before HE would let her date; actually my father had said he would *think* about it when she turned sixteen, if he 'approved of the young man'. There was no way she wanted to get in my father's bad books right now – although as far as I was concerned she had to work real hard to get in his bad books. Jo-Ann had been sneaking out to meet old pimple-face at McDonald's and I had proof she had gone to two movies with him, so I had her.

'Just wait, Margaret Cruickshank, just wait,' she whispered, real fierce, and even a little frightened. She really wanted to date pimple-face: 'I'll never ever ever call you Harriet again, so there.'

'Night Jo-Ann,' I said, and threw myself, clothes and all, into bed.

But it was the beginning of the end really. Although we had our new 'Freedom', there was a lot of anger between us all. Everyone was taking the game too seriously, and we – Zulma and I – just couldn't figure out why, or how, the owners or dogs had discovered the first 'Freedom'. Zulma was sure, doubly and triply sure, that it was Ti-cush.

'Is who else?' she asked me. 'Is who else?'

'But how did she find out?'

'You want know what me think? Me think she did follow you dat morning to "Freedom" – remember you did tell she you wasn't going play dat day, but you was going to baby-sit Sandro – remember? She know you have to leave your house and go to "Freedom", and me sure as dere is a God above, dat is what she do, me will bet me bottom dollar on it.'

'Hmmmm, maybe you're right.'

'Me *know* me right. Once she see where you went, she hot-foot it to she house so that when Pina call she to say dey leaving "slavery", she could answer de phone. And you want know something else too, me sure is she who stirring up all dese problems now. She jealous of you.'

It was too late for the game, I felt it in my bones. It had begun to spill over into the regular school day. Every day there was at least one fight that had to do with the game – recess time, after school – you name it, there they were calling each other names. We had to stop playing, I told the group. They wanted to continue. Since I had started the game, I didn't think I could just drop out, so we continued; but I was worried, and my heart wasn't in it.

My mother had told me that the teachers were talking and asking questions. I had to pretend that I didn't know anything. One day on the playground, I heard Maria Rao, a slave, call another kid, I think it was Harry Bradshaw, a dog – 'a dirty, rotten, dog, who bit poor people, who were trying to be free'. I tried to settle it, but they wanted to fight it out. Somebody else, Angela Augustine, got called a "no-good slave", and I'm sure it was Gino Di Cecco who threatened to set his dog on her. Parents began to call the school to complain about name-calling – this again from my mother.

I was in the office the day the Browns came to school to complain. Their families, they said, were descended from Maroons *on both sides*; the Maroons had fought to be free and fought again to keep that freedom. They didn't want their daughter, Pat, being called a slave, by no one. They had never been slaves! Never! I deliberately hung around the office to hear what else they knew.

Through my mother, I heard about the Di Caros who complained about their son waking up at nights screaming about not wanting to be caught by dogs, and only wanting to get to freedom. He had said it was something he was studying at school.

It was through her also that I heard about Chrissie Campbell. Chrissie thinks she's God's gift to the world and so do her parents; I had always been surprised that she had wanted to play, but play she did, and as a dog, which she loved. Chrissie had taken to howling like a dog when she was excited, which really broke me up. She had told her parents she was studying a play at school in which she had the part of a dog. They wanted her to have another part; she was very highly strung, they said, and they wanted her to use her ballet and drama training in some other way. Even my mother had a laugh about Chrissie, who was always dressed like a model (my mother liked that), howling like a dog.

It was Sandro, Pina's little brother, who brought things to a head and ended the game for us. I had just taken a message from my teacher to the office, right after the second bell, and so I saw the whole thing. Pina, her mother *and* her father were dragging Sandro kicking and screaming up the stairs – he was yelling his head off about his FREE PAPERS, and how he didn't have to go to school because he was free. They finally got him inside the school, where he lay on the floor in the lobby and screamed. Pina looked at me, I looked at her, and we knew something soft and wet was going to hit the fan, and we were all going to get spattered.

Mr and Mrs Francesconi were mad as hell: with each other, with Sandro and, from the way they were talking with the Principal, Mrs Chalmers. Mrs Chalmers was trying to calm them down, but she wasn't succeeding; Mrs Francesconi said that she was going to go to her local school trustee *and* her Member of Parliament, because the school was not doing anything to help her son. I didn't know this then but only found out later from Pina, that this was not the first time Sandro had done his FREE PAPERS trick to get out of school – he was a smart kid that Sandro, milking his sister of her pocket-money to keep quiet and now trying to get out of school.

'Get everyone together,' I whispered to Pina, 'at recess time,' and I went back to my class.

At recess time we met over at the baseball diamond: 'Look guys,' I said, 'we've got to stop the game – no more – it's no fun any longer and we're getting in trouble.' At first some kids said no way, but Pina, Zulma, and I managed to show them why we

84

had to stop. By the end of recess, I was feeling really happy and relieved; the bloody game was over. The feeling didn't last long though – when I got back in, Mrs Chalmers sent for me. My heart was going so fast I thought it would jump right through my mouth. I knew why she wanted me.

I sat facing her in her office and she smiled at me; I wondered if she would still be smiling at me after we talked. I liked her quite a bit, she seemed kind.

'Hello Margaret.'

I said hello back, and she pushed a piece of paper toward me.

'Read this and tell me what it means.'

It was a note, a short one, written in pencil on a torn piece of paper. I read: 'Margaret Cruickshank alias Harriet Tubman knows all about it.' I read it again and looked at her.

'Yes Mrs Chalmers?'

'Is your name Harriet Tubman?'

'Not Harriet Tubman, just Harriet. My friends and my mum have been calling me Harriet.'

'Why?'

I explained my wanting to change my name.

'And what is the "all" you know?'

I decided to make a clean break of it all. The game was over, I was sick and tired of it, and fed up with all the kids. So I talked, and told Mrs Chalmers everything – well not everything – I didn't tell her about our late night run from the police, but everything apart from that. And she listened. Her face didn't show anything when I was done and I thought: this is it, I'm going to be thrown out.

Then she said, 'Do you really wish to change your name to Harriet, Margaret?'

I was surprised at the question, I wasn't expecting it. 'Yes I think so . . .'

'You know you can change your name legally?'

I nodded, remembering what my mum had said. 'My dad will never let me though. Margaret is his mother's name.'

All she said was, 'Hmmmm.'

'And now – about the Underground Railroad Game.' My heart fell. 'You organised and planned the whole thing yourself?'

I nodded again. I didn't want to take all the 'glory', but I didn't want to get anyone in trouble, so I didn't mention any other names.

'You know it cannot continue.'

'We decided to end it today, Mrs Chalmers.'

She smiled. 'That's good. I don't disapprove of the game – it's a good idea, a very good idea – maybe we could use it in a school play, but it's having too many unfortunate repercussions.'

She asked me if I knew what she meant by repercussions. I said yes – 'Sandro Francesconi.' She smiled again.

'Right. Now I want to meet with your parents.' I didn't say anything but she saw my face. 'You don't want me to talk with them, is that it?'

'No Mrs Chalmers.'

'Well you know Marg . . . I mean Harriet, it's going to be impossible to keep it from the staff and the parents, like the Francesconis. We owe them an explanation, don't you think so?'

'Yes,' I said, my voice real low, 'but not my parents, especially my father.'

'But Harriet, your mother works here, she's bound to find out. I don't think I can do anything else but tell them. I'm not trying to get you into trouble, you know that. There were other children involved, and I respect your not wanting to call their names and get them in trouble; but we all have to meet and talk it through, and explain to the parents what the causes of the name-calling, and nightmares are all about. Their parents and your parents are already involved.'

She was right and I knew it, but I also knew my father. I could write his speech – Coloured People would be mentioned a lot – so would be setting a bad example, and on and on. 'Yes Mrs Chalmers,' was all I could say.

After school we all met at the baseball diamond. I told the others that Mrs Chalmers knew about the game and that she would be wanting to talk to their parents. There was a lot of talk about that; I could see they were worried.

'It's cool guys – she's not angry, but since some parents already know something's up, she wants to . . . *has* to talk to everyone.'

'How did she find out?' someone asked.

'Someone squealed,' I said and told them about the note. There was more talk – a lot more talk about that and who it could be.

'I suppose you think I had something to do with this,' said Ti-cush. She was obviously in a fighting mood.

'I didn't say that, Ti-cush, but did you?'

We stared at each other, her face red and angry, mine serious.

'Go stuff yourself and your game!' she said. 'Anyway, it was a real stupid game – with all those slaves and dogs and I'm glad you got caught – so there.' She spat on the ground, turned and walked off looking real hurt and angry. I looked at her as she walked off; I still liked her, hoped we could be friends again sometime in the future.

'Me did tell you so – me did tell you so – she was a cross 'pon de game, nothing but a cross.'

We looked at each other and smiled. 'You were right Zulma.'

The group was breaking up; everyone drifting away, slaves, and guides were now friends with slave-owners and dogs. Now the game was over, everyone was remembering the good times and talking about them.

'Hey, remember when Frankie brought his dog?'

'Yeah, the dog that didn't bark.' I could hear the laughter, as Zulma and I walked across the playground.

'Frankie said he only barked when he got excited – he was one excited dog.'

'I liked being the decoy best of all,' someone else said, 'with my FREE PAPERS. Remember the look on Ti-cush's face that day?' More laughter.

Someone shouted, 'Long live the Underground Railroad.' Others joined in: 'Long live the Underground Railroad.'

15

It was my turn to be right, about Mrs Chalmers talking to my parents, to HIM at least. I didn't see any point in getting him riled up with me beforehand, so I didn't tell him why Mrs Chalmers wanted to see them.

When they got back, nobody said anything to me. This silent treatment made it worse, but I knew I would hear about it soon enough, no doubt at dinner time. And so it was.

'What's this Mrs Chalmers tells me about an Underground Railroad Game?'

'Didn't she explain?'

'Yes, she did. She also said she thought it was quite impressive that you had thought it up all by yourself – that we should be proud of you.'

'But you aren't. Right?'

'Don't put words in my mouth girl,' he said. 'What I want to know is why you were wasting your time playing some silly game, when you should have been studying.'

'But I don't have to study any more Dad. I'm doing well, and the game was on Saturdays. I don't study on Saturdays.'

'Mrs Chalmers also said that parents were calling the school all upset about the effect this game was having on their children.'

'It's all over now, Dad.'

'That's not the point. The first thing they're going to say is "There they go again, those Coloured People – always causing trouble". How many times do I have to tell you that you have to be careful, people are very quick to believe the worst about us.'

'It was only a game, Dad,' and I muttered under my breath that people would think whatever they wanted to think about us no matter what we did.

'What was that?' he asked. I didn't repeat it – didn't say anything more. 'And what's all this nonsense about changing your name? Isn't Margaret good enough for you? It's a perfectly good name, it was your grandmother's and her mother's before her.' He turned to my mum: 'I blame you, Tina, for all this stupidness about names. You encouraged her in this foolishness.'

My mum looked like she was going to throw her food at him. Then her face came over all closed and stubborn looking, but she didn't say anything. HE went on: 'You children these days have too much freedom, and the school is to blame for it. If you had some work – real work – to do, you wouldn't have time to run around playing Underground Railroad Games.' He stopped talking for a while; took a drink of water, and continued.

I can see it all like a film in my mind: he put down his glass, made this gross sound in his throat and I knew what was coming. I shut my eyes real tight, curled my hands into two fists, and wished and willed with all my might that he would continue talking about Coloured People. I never thought I would wish to hear him talk about his favourite subject, but I did then – I wanted him to go on and on forever about Coloured People, because then I would never have to hear the words 'Barbados! Summer! Grandmother! Next year!' The words hung there in the air over the dining-table. I could see them, even though I had my eyes shut. I didn't move a muscle.

'Did you hear me girl? Do you understand what I have just said?'

I refused to open my eyes. As long as I kept them shut I wouldn't have to face what he was saying; that's what I thought, so I kept them closed, real tight.

'Open your eyes and stop being stupid.' It was impossible to close my eyes any tighter, but I did until I saw all kinds of colours dancing before them.

'Do you see what I mean Tina? Do you see where all your foolishness has got her?' My mother didn't answer. He didn't expect her to reply to him. To me, he said: 'You'll have this nonsense knocked out of you if it's the last thing I do, and it will happen in Barbados. And I'll repeat what I just said so that you understand clearly what is going to happen: You will . . .'

'No!' I screamed at him, it just came out. I pushed back my chair, knocking it over. 'I'm not going, I'm not going,' I yelled, 'you can go if *you* want, but I'm not going to Barbados or anywhere, this is my home. And I'm not coloured either – I'm black, black, black!'

'Sit down and be quiet.' He banged his fist on the table and everything jumped – like the dominoes, I remembered, thinking.

'No, I don't want to sit down – and you can't make me.' I turned to my mother. 'Mum, you said I could go to camp again this year, you said so.' My mum was useless; she was crying and crying, and she wasn't even the one being sent away. 'You both said so,' I said. 'Mum, please, help me.'

'Your father knows what's best for you Margaret.'

'He doesn't, he doesn't, he doesn't!' Then my legs crumbled, like someone had kicked them out from under me. I collapsed – onto my chair; I hadn't known but my sister had picked it up for me. I owed her one for that.

'You're being extremely rude and not helping matters at all.' His face was like a rock as he said these words. 'Furthermore, young lady, every Saturday, in addition to your other chores, I want you to clean my car – inside and out. That should keep you busy. Your mother is to know where you are *at all times*. Tina do you understand that? You really haven't been doing your job you know.' My mum nodded.

I made one last effort, swallowed my pride. I didn't care if I lost face: 'Please Dad, can't we talk about this? I promise I'll be better. I'll do whatever you want me to do.'

'There is no more discussion Margaret. Your behaviour just now has convinced me of that. There are what? . . . three more weeks of school. After that you're going to Barbados to your grandmother's. Oh and . . .'

I didn't wait for him to finish. I scraped back my chair, got up and walked out of the room. I heard him call to me to come back, but I just kept walking up to my room. I went and sat on my bed; it was then I noticed that I was clenching my teeth real tight. I could hear HIM and my mother talking still, not the actual words, just the sound of voices. I was sure they were talking about me.

I didn't belong anywhere, nobody wanted me, they all wanted to be rid of me. That was how I felt sitting on the bed, thinking of what my father had just said.

'Harriet? Harriet?' Believe it or not, it was Jo-Ann, my sister. She came in and put her arm around me: 'I don't want you to go to Barbados, even though we don't get along. Sometimes Dad's really too much. He told Mum after you left, that he didn't want you being called Harriet, but I'll call you Harriet.'

I smiled a little: 'Thanks Jo, but it doesn't matter now,' and I fell back on my bed. I didn't want her to see the tears in my eyes. 'Thanks Jo. I just want to be alone now O.K.?'

'O.K.' At the door, she turned and told me I could borrow *any* of her make-up and *any* of her clothes. She was really feeling sorry for me – Jo-Ann never offered to lend me *anything*. It was too bad, I thought, she didn't have any money to lend me and Zulma. Make-up and clothes weren't going to get me out of that house and away from parents who didn't want me in any case.

16

I was going to run away – with Zulma – I had made up my mind. HE wasn't going to send me off like baggage, and definitely not to his mother in Barbados. Where were we going to run to? Zulma and I spent long hours talking about it. I didn't know a lot of French, so I was worried about going to Montreal. I thought of Vancouver, or New York. Zulma just wanted to go home to her gran, but felt that anywhere far away from her stepfather, was a good second choice. We talked a lot and did nothing. We were both nervous and talking helped. At least it made us think we were doing something – planning, organising – whatever.

We needed some money before we left, so we both put our names in at the McDonald's at St Clair and Christie. Zulma told me she was going to say her prayers for us: 'You watch,' she said, 'when me pray, me prayers always get answered.'

'You better pray my mother has a change of heart about giving me some money' (I had told Zulma exactly what the situation was with my mother and the money she held for me), 'and that HE changes his mind about sending me to Barbados.'

Neither of those things happened, but Zulma's prayers were answered, in a really strange way. On the second Saturday after I had been given my 'deportation order' (that's how I liked to think of it sometimes), I was sitting in his car. I was supposed to be cleaning it, but I was pretending to drive it. I sat in the driver's seat and played around with the steering-wheel. I was at the Grand Prix, and had just come around the final bend in the course; the crowd was going crazy over me and my driving, they were screaming and yelling my name as I came down the last drag! Hell! My mother was looking at me through the living-room window. My father did not like me playing around with the steering-wheel, and I didn't want any more hassles with him.

I went around to the passenger side, opened the door and began to clean. I took out the mat and shook it, then I vacuumed where the mat was, and the upholstery. I bent down to put the mat back the way it was, but I couldn't get it to lie flat. Just where it went under the seat it buckled. I stuck my hand under the mat to feel for whatever it was that was making the bump. I felt around and my fingers closed around what felt like a wad of papers. I pulled it out: 'Hell,' I said, 'stupid Canadian Tire coupons,' and I threw them on the seat while I lay the mat flat. I picked up the coupons to throw them in the garbage bag and my heart went all funny, and my legs got weak and rubbery. I sat down in the passenger seat and unrolled the Canadian Tire 'money' – except that it wasn't Canadian Tire money. It was seven hundred dollars of real live money.

I knew right away where it had come from: my mum's partners savings scheme. My first thought was that maybe she had left it for me to find, but I knew that was silly. She had dropped it, it had got wedged, somehow, under the mat and I had found it. I don't know how long it was missing; it couldn't have been more than a week, since it hadn't been there when I cleaned the car a week ago. I also knew that we wouldn't ever hear about the missing money in my home. My mother would never give my father the chance to say 'I told you so' about what he called her 'primitive' savings scheme. My mother would definitely keep the loss to herself.

Here I was now, sitting holding seven one-hundred dollar bills in my hands. Two of my mother's friends must have dropped out – I was sure it used to be nine of them that were involved in the savings plan. I turned the money over and over looking at the bills closely; I had never seen so much money in all my life.

When did the idea first come to me? I don't know, but once it had, it stuck to me like crazy glue. No matter how much I talked to myself, said it was crazy and wrong – that it was my mum's money and I should go inside right now and give it to her at once; that I would roast in hell, never get to heaven; be tarred and feathered by HIM – no matter how much I thought those thoughts, the idea just hung on in my mind: to use the money to help me and Zulma run away. I could even pay for Zulma to go home to her gran. I could go with her! It would be a loan of course. My mum could pay herself back from Mrs Blewchamp's money, or from my baby bonus savings. It wasn't stealing, just a short-term loan – that's what the banks called it, and my mother was the banker.

Another voice said to me: 'Bankers know when they are making loans; your mother doesn't have a choice in this loan, and if she did, wouldn't loan you the money. You have already asked her, and she has said no.' This voice came out of somebody dressed in white and who looked like God. How does God look? I don't know, but this person was real serious and looked like my father and mother and Mrs Chalmers all rolled into one; and to make it worse, the person was pointing right at me, like the priest pointed at me one day in church and told me to stop talking.

I got out of the car. I had to talk to someone – a grown-up, someone kind and generous, who would tell me to forget that pointing finger and listen to the other voice – the voice of the bank manager, wanting to make me a loan. Wasn't that just great, a bank manager and God having an argument. The bank manager would say: 'But we can make fifteen per cent interest per day on the loan, and that would make you much richer God, just think how many more souls you could save.' God would reply: 'I'm not interested in money, but in this little girl's soul, I don't want her to burn in hell.' I shook my head and laughed, was I going crazy? I didn't believe in hell or any of that stuff; I wasn't sure about God, but even feeling this way I still felt that there was something not quite right about what I wanted – more than anything else in this world – to do.

Mrs B's face was suddenly there in my mind, full of smiles offering me milk and cookies. She'll understand I thought, she's bound to, and if anyone can argue with God, or a bank manager, it's Mrs B. I put the money in my pocket and went inside.

'Mum, I've done the car. Can I go over and see Mrs B, she said I could come over any Saturday for cookies.'

'O.K., but be back in time for supper.'

Mrs B had made honey cake and cookies that Saturday. 'Come on in,' she said. 'Looking for your daddy? He's not here today, honey; I think they're playing at Sam Wilson's place today.'

'No, no, Mrs B, I just want to talk.'

'Well talk away then. I just have these cookie sheets to clean, but I can listen while I do that. Have a slice of cake and some cookies while you talk. Nothing like a bit of food to help loosen the tongue . . . what about some milk, honey?'

I nodded, took a deep breath and began. 'Mrs B if you found some money and really really needed it, but knew who it belonged to, and that person had money for you – money that was yours, and you used that money, but wanted them to take it from your money which they had – would that be stealing? In my head the bank manager voice says it's a loan, but another voice says no, it's wrong.'

Mrs B just stood and watched me while I talked. When I had stopped talking, she didn't say a word. She washed her hands, dried them and sat down at the table.

'Now Margaret, how about if you begin at the beginning,' she smiled at me, 'and slow, real slow this time. Whose money do you have, and why do you think it might be stealing? And eat up honey, no wonder you're so nervous.' I took a small bite of a cookie, and I looked at her right in the eye.

'You've got to promise, Mrs B, not to tell anyone, because I might get in more trouble than I am already.'

'More trouble? Are you in trouble? You too young to have troubles; trouble is what we adults do to each other.'

'Say you promise Mrs B.'

She looked anxious now, like she was worried for me, then: 'I promise Margaret, but you have to promise something in return. You must promise to let me help you, if I can. It's not right you should be so worried and troubled.'

I promised.

Then I explained everything to Mrs B. It was such a relief to talk – about my parents – especially my dad not liking me; about my name, about the game and what had happened, and about Zulma. Mrs B listened, her whole body listened to what I had to say, and when I was done she didn't say anything. I sat there playing with the cookies on the plate.

'You said something about money that was yours, but which was being saved.' I explained about Mrs Blewchamp, the baby bonus cheques and how my mother had refused to give me any of it to help Zulma.

She still didn't say anything, then she asked me what I wanted to do with the money.

At first I didn't say anything, didn't look at her, nothing. Then I took a real deep breath and said: 'Buy Zulma a ticket to Tobago.'

'And how about you, Margaret? What do *you* want to do?'

I looked down at my plate again. All kinds of thoughts were going through my mind, but most of all I didn't want to go to Barbados to live with my grandmother, and if my parents didn't want me living with them, then . . . 'Go with Zulma, maybe,' I muttered.

'Look at me Margaret,' Mrs B's voice was low, but real firm, 'look at me, child, and tell me what *you* want to do.' I looked up and met her eyes, and she refused to let me look away. 'I can't help you if I don't know what *you* want to do . . .' I nodded and she went on, 'and you promised to let me help you.'

Now that I held enough money in my hands to do what I

wanted to do, I was feeling really scared, even to face up to what I had wanted and planned for so long.

'I want to buy Zulma and me tickets, and go to Tobago.' I said this more firmly now. 'Zulma says her gran would love to have me.'

'There now, child,' Mrs B smiled at me, 'that wasn't too bad now, saying that.' It was funny, but I didn't mind Mrs B calling me child – it didn't make me feel small – just safe and protected. When HE called me child, I wanted to yell and scream at him that I was no child.

I looked at Mrs B's face, it was now serious and almost sad looking. We just sat there together for a while not saying anything. Then she said:

'You know what you're saying is that you want to leave your mammy and daddy.'

'Yes Mrs B,' I could feel a big lump in my throat, which I tried swallowing, 'and I want you to help me and Zulma.'

Mrs B suddenly went loose, it was funny, like a big sack or balloon losing its air. She covered her face with both hands, then wiped them over her closed eyes, as if she was trying to wipe away something. She just sat there staring, not at me, but at something only she could see. I was getting anxious and thinking how grown-ups always acted strange, no matter how nice they were.

Mrs B said she would help me, but here she was just sitting there, staring in front of her like she was seeing a ghost. Then she shifted her body, and sort of moaned and sighed, but the sound didn't come from her throat but from her whole body. It was like her whole body had groaned. I didn't even realise I was holding my breath until I too let out a sort of sigh. Then Mrs B began talking.

17

'I wasn't much older than you Margaret, when I ran away . . .'
I could feel the effort it was for her to speak, it was like she was
pushing the words out. 'My family lived in Mississippi . . .
Mammy died having her thirteenth child . . . my father?' She
asked herself the question: 'He'd taken off with some fancy
high-coloured woman as soon as the last shovel full of dirt hit
Mammy's coffin. Us children were shared out like so much
baggage, between friends and relatives: cheap labour, the
cheapest you could find in a land of cheap labour.' She laughed
– a sound that was real different from what her laughter used to
sound like. 'And believe me when I say there was a lot of labour
to be done in those days.

'Aunt Cleo was her name, the one I ended up with. She took
an instant dislike to me – maybe I wasn't pretty enough, too
scrawny – huh,' she made a sound and her whole body shook,
but she wasn't laughing. 'Yes, I was pretty scrawny in those
days . . . maybe too black for her, who knows, but Auntie Cleo
didn't like me. Maybe I reminded her, of something she didn't
want to be reminded of, she was sort of light brown and had
what I call pretensions, you know what I mean.' She looked
directly at me as if she was surprised to see me there.

'Pretensions and aspirations for herself and her daughters,
but the wrong sort . . . I was to help her fulfil those. Huh!' She
stopped talking, folded her arms over her bosom, and shook her
head. 'I came close to death in that first year I lived with her –
pleurisy, pneumonia – as long as I could move, she worked me,
and when I couldn't move, or wouldn't, she would flog me.

Sometimes I just lay in bed, too sick and too tired to move. She called the preacher several times for me, she was so sure I was going to die, and all she could talk of was the cost of the burial.

'The last time I was ill – double pneumonia – I heard my Aunt Cleo outside the shed where I slept, haggling with a neighbour about the cheapest coffin he could build, and demanding to know whether he had any old pieces of wood lying around that he could use for a coffin; a pine coffin, she felt, was much too expensive for me. Mind you, the cheapest coffin you could get in those days was pine, but that was too good for me. That was what made up my mind, her talking as if I was already dead, and wanting the cheapest wood for my coffin.'

Her eyes focused on me again, as if she was seeing me for the first time. Her face was wet, not with tears, sweat maybe? Cold sweat. I began to feel cold too, although the kitchen was warm. I wrapped my arms around myself. I didn't really want to listen, but Mrs B's words wouldn't let me go – I felt caught by them – like they had taken the place of my words. Somewhere I knew that Mrs B had to tell me what she was telling me, and she told it like it was the first time she had ever told the story. Maybe it was – and I had to listen, but I felt that I didn't want to hear any more – how people were cruel to each other.

Mrs B must have noticed something because her voice was suddenly dry; she talked like she was reading a shopping list, a boring one too. 'I ran away at fourteen . . . Lying in that bed, I decided that Aunt Cleo or no Aunt Cleo, I was going to run as soon as I got better, and that anything had to be better than the hard work, the floggings, and starvation. I jumped a train – ran north to Detroit where I had some relatives.' She stopped talking. This time she gave a real chuckle, and I felt better when I heard it; it was much more like what I was used to hearing from her.

She laughed out loud, and shook her head like she didn't quite believe her thoughts. 'Before I left Aunt Cleo, I took everything I could carry away from there easily – every piece of silver and jewellery – she didn't have much of that, jewellery I mean, but she had a few pieces of really good silver; that, and every penny I could lay my hands on, I took, and left one night when they were all out at a neighbour's. She used to keep her money sewed up in her mattress. I unpicked it all and took it, all five-hundred and ninety-six dollars and fifty cents; that was a hell of a lot those days.' Mrs B smiled again; she was happy remembering what she had done. 'Lord I would have given anything to have seen her face when she found me and the money and the silver gone – well not anything – not my freedom. No, not that.'

She looked at me again with that funny expression, like she was surprised to see me there; then she looked around the kitchen as if she was even more surprised to be there. 'What I did was wrong, very wrong . . . I know that, knew it back then. But she stole my health, my strength . . . and my youth . . .' Her face was a deep grey now. I was getting real scared – what if she got sick? Her body had collapsed even further into itself, she looked like she didn't have any bones, like she was all flesh. If I could put a colour to her voice, it would have been the same rough, grey colour as her face. 'I figured it was a fair exchange – my youth for Aunt Cleo's money.' She laughed again, pulled herself up and her skeleton came back. Mrs B had a real good circus act making her skeleton go away and come back like that, I thought. Her laughter was like a hoarse bark, it scraped at my ears.

'I didn't find them – my relatives – for two years, but I was right, life was better than at Aunt Cleo's. I worked in white people's kitchens, and I worked hard. Sometimes I had to leave when the men got too fast and forward, and the women turned blind and rude, but I wasn't flogged, and I could leave work at the end of the day. I went back to school, and got a couple more grades. The jobs improved a bit; then I met Mr Billings, from Canada. In those days it sounded so different and exciting – "from Canada".'

She was smiling now and her eyes were bright. I could tell

101

that the memories, the bad ones, were still close, but the memory of her courtship (that's what she called it) and life in Canada won out.

'We were such romantic fools in those days . . .' She laughed, almost like me and Zulma. 'Anyway, here I am in Canada for these last thirty-two years – Lord that's a long time.'

She pushed herself up to her feet and went back to cleaning the cookie sheets, laughing quietly to herself. 'You should have shut me up, Margaret – all that going on to you about my life, when you've got your own problems.'

I didn't say anything, just sat there propping my chin on my hand, and thought how strange and confusing grown-ups were. First they talk and talk, things you don't really want to hear; then they say you should have shut them up . . . and if you had, they would have said you were being rude.

Mrs B came and sat next to me. 'What's up child . . . ? I didn't upset you did I, with all my talking?'

I shook my head but still didn't say anything.

'Well what's the matter? You just sitting there propping sorrow as we used to say. C'mon, tell Bertha what's bothering you.'

'It's just – just that my problems are so – so nothing compared to yours . . . I shouldn't have come and bothered you.'

Mrs B pulled her chair closer to mine and put her arms around me. 'You poor child. What a stupid old woman I am, not noticing what I was doing to you – forgive me child, forgive me, but I couldn't help myself. When I heard you wanted to run away, everything just came rushing back so clear and fresh; it was like I was there again, at Aunt Cleo's, just wanting to get out. But you're not to think that means your problems aren't important. Don't ever let anybody tell you what's worrying you ought not to worry you – because you're not anyone else, and they're not you, isn't that so?'

I was sitting with my head against Mrs B's bosom – I nodded. 'I remember,' she went on, in a low gentle voice,

102

'Mammy used to say to us, "Try and never measure or judge anyone, but if you have to, make sure and measure the hills she done walk up and down, the valleys she done come through, the rivers she cross, and the shoes she wearing – if she wearing shoes at all – to come to where she is." You understand what I mean by that Margaret, that my crosses, which are long gone in any case, are no reflection on yours. You are Margaret, and I am Bertha, and from what you've told me you have every cause to feel unhappy.'

'Will you help us to run away then?'

'I don't know child. Is that the best way to help you?' I was now facing her. 'That might be breaking the law. Hold on, don't go looking so unhappy, remember I promised to help you. Isn't there any way of reasoning with your father?'

'No, Mrs Chalmers talked to him and it didn't make any difference. She wasn't even angry with me about the game; all she wanted was to tell him that they could change my name legally, and it was after that he decided to send me to Barbados.'

'Hmmm, I see.' Mrs B's face was serious. I stared at her, willing her to give me the answer I wanted. 'Let's deal with the money,' she said. 'You say you're sure it belongs to your mother? D'you know for sure it was her turn to get the money this month? Maybe she collected it for someone else in the group?'

'It's hers, Mrs B, I know it. I remember her telling a friend on the phone that it was her turn to get it this month, and that she was thinking of buying a water-bed for her and my dad. She also said she was thinking of paying for some modelling lessons for Jo-Ann . . .'

'O.K., so you know it's hers, and you want to know whether it's stealing if you keep it, since she has money of yours.' I nodded. 'Well if you could pay her back right away, it wouldn't be stealing; but if you could do that, then you would have the money to do what you want,' I nodded again, 'and you wouldn't have to ask yourself whether you're stealing, because you wouldn't have to, or wouldn't think of keeping your mammy's money, right?' I didn't say anything.

'Until you pay her back that money, Margaret, you're keeping it without her permission, and since it's not yours, in my book that is stealing . . .' I didn't move, I slowly raised my eyes and met hers, full of concern. 'Even though she has money that is yours, you are a child and she has the right to keep that money for you until you come of age. I know how mad that makes you, how frustrating it is, *and* I also believe that parents can be wrong sometimes as well.'

'But can't it be a loan, a kind of long-term loan?'

'Yes, but how's she to know it's a loan, you're not going to rush home and tell her you're making a loan of her seven-hundred dollars, are you?'

'No, I couldn't do that.' I didn't say anything for a while, then I said, 'But I so want to help Zulma get back to Tobago. I promised her that, Mrs B – and I want to keep that promise. She misses her gran so much.'

'But child you're both children, she'll understand if you can't keep it.'

'But don't you see, with me gone in the summer, there will be no one to help her. Her stepfather hates her; her mother's too scared to go against him and help her. What's she going to do? She won't even have me to talk to any more.'

'Yes, I see what you mean, I see what you mean . . . Well I'm going to have to think about all this . . . and do a bit of praying as well, I suppose.'

'There's only another week before school's out though Mrs B.'

'That's all right, it won't take long. Also I want to meet Zulma, may as well get to know who I'm helping eh?'

'Does that mean you're going to help us run away?'

'Not so fast honey child. I didn't say that. I said I got to think and pray about it, part of my thinking is meeting Zulma.'

'Oh great! You know what?'

'No, what?'

'You're a modern-day Harriet Tubman.'

'Well I may be a Harriet, but there's nothing about you that reminds me of a slave.'

'Slaves were much worse off than we are . . . but Mrs B sometimes I feel so helpless, not having any rights or power. Slaves must have felt something like that, don't you think?'

Mrs B laughed and nodded. 'You're quite right, quite right. I used to feel like that a lot when I was growing up. All right now, scram. When are you going to bring Zulma over?'

'Tomorrow after church – in the afternoon – about two o'clock?'

'That's fine. Mr Billings sleeps then, so we can talk.'

'See you then Mrs B.'

'Here take some cookies with you, you hardly ate any. Oh, I almost forgot – what are you going to do with that money – return it to your mother? Have you decided?'

I stopped at the doorway of the kitchen. Mrs B's question, the question in her eyes, and the question inside me, all the same question, confronted me. I looked down and shook my head. 'I promised to help Zulma,' I said, 'and I'm going to help her. I know it's stealing, but I think helping Zulma is more important than getting a water-bed or buying modelling lessons for Jo-Ann.'

'You're quite a girl, Margaret, quite a girl. You've got more courage than most adults I know. O.K., where's the money now?'

'Here.' I shoved my hand in my pocket of my jeans, pulled out a wad of notes and held them out to Mrs B.

'You should leave it here, child, and not go wandering all over the place with seven-hundred dollars.'

'Thank you Mrs B. I really didn't want to keep it with me when I went back home.' I put the money on the kitchen table and left.

I thought of making up an excuse about not feeling well, to get out of being at the dinner table, but I didn't want to call too much attention to myself, so I decided against it.

18

I was sure my mum had noticed that she had lost the money, but she wouldn't say anything. At dinner, I stared at her, wondering why she was being so quiet. I wanted to say something – anything to her – to tell her not to worry, that I was only borrowing the money, but I wasn't of course. I wished it was HIS money. I would have felt a lot – a hell of a lot – better.

Thinking of Zulma made me feel better. I had to remember that I was helping Zulma, that made me feel less selfish and cruel. When I told Zulma about it, about finding the money and being able to help her, we were walking along St Clair, on our way to Mrs B. She stopped – her face got this funny look, both happy and sad at the same time, like she was going to laugh and cry.

'Me don't believe it – it too good to be true,' she said. 'It can't be real.'

'It is, Zulma, it is – Mrs B has the money – she's keeping it for me.'

'Real live money?'

I laughed. 'Yep, all seven-hundred dollars' worth of real live money.'

'Oh Lord God,' she said, 'I know me prayers always get answer, but I scared, Harriet, real scared. What if dey find out, and your mother – what about she?'

'I know, I know. I hate to make her worried, but it's kind of a loan, isn't it, because she has all this money of mine. Mrs B says it's not really a loan – it's really stealing.'

'Stealing? Gran always say I should never, never do dat – dat what I get must come to me in de right way, or not at all. You think dis money come to we in the right way, Margaret?'

'Oh I don't know, Zulma, I don't know . . . All I know is that I want to help you . . . go back to your gran . . . and I don't want to go to Barbados. They were going to pay for me to go to Barbados, so I'm saving them that fare, aren't I? What d'you think?'

She and I looked at each other; we were both worried. 'I don't feel good about it, Zulma, and I wish I did. I wish I did.'

I saw Zulma take a deep breath and squeeze her eyes shut – tightly. I reached out and put my hand on her shoulder.

'You o.k. Zulma?'

'Uh huh – is just that when me think of not going back to Gran, of staying here, me feel this tightness here.' She pointed to her chest. 'When me think of you having the money for me to go, it sort of get loose, and then it get tight again, when me think of you having to give it back and me staying here and not seeing Gran, oh . . .' She took another deep breath, and I could feel tears making my eyes prickly. I put my arms around her. 'We going go, Zulma, we going go,' I wanted to say it in her language, 'we both going go to your gran, trust me. I did promise you, remember?' She nodded.

'Me don't want get you in trouble.'

'I *am* already in trouble Zulma – with HIM, but Mrs B's going to help us. Come on let's go and see her. She's bound to have something good for us to eat.'

She did too, peach cobbler and ice cream.

While we ate, Mrs B questioned Zulma about her parents and how she came to be in Canada. Zulma talked and ate and talked some more.

'Do you really want to go back?'

'Yes ma'am. Is only because of Margaret – I mean Harriet – that me like being here. Me stepfather don't like me, and me mother don't know what to do about it. Me miss me gran and Tobago, but me don't want get Margaret in trouble.'

'And things aren't getting any better?'

107

'No ma'am, worse. Me didn't tell you dis yet, Margaret, but we had another quarrel last night. He hit me mother again, and when me tell he not to hit she, he turn and slap me; then he tell me mother, she have to find somewhere else for me to live – that he not having no child who think she is a woman living in same house with he. Me ask she to let me go back to Gran, but she don't want me to because she feel Gran going to be angry with she and tell she that she should never have bring me up here. Me think she feel sending me back to Gran is like saying she fail. She also think that the education better up here than in Tobago.'

'Baloney! How can you learn if you're not happy?'

'Me don't know where she would get de money from to send me back in any case, she don't have any of she own. She give it all to me stepfather.'

'Now that's a mistake, a very serious mistake. Once a man begins to control your money, he's not going to want to stop there. Next it's your body, then your mind. Uh uh, that's a mistake.'

She shook her head and went on as if talking to herself: 'How some women can be so foolish is beyond me,' then she caught herself, and realised that she had an audience. 'I'm sorry, child, no offence meant to your mother. Tell me, Zulma, if Margaret here doesn't do, or can't do, for some reason, what she says she wants to do, what are you going to do?'

'Run away ma'am.' Zulma was real cool about the way she explained everything to Mrs B. 'Me and Margaret talked about it. Is the only way me mother going know that me not happy, and that me don't want to live with she if she living with me stepfather – and that me want to go back to Gran.'

'Where you going to run to?'

'Don't know, ma'am, but me know lots of kids go to Montreal – maybe me will get put in a foster home – even dat will be better than where me is now.'

'It's not easy out there for young girls, you know.'

'Me know dat, ma'am.'

'Specially young, black girls.'

'Me know dat too ma'am.'

'And you've got no other relatives here at all Zulma?'

'No ma'am, none at all.'

'Hmmmm. Here,' she said, getting up, 'have some more peach cobbler.'

She sat back down at the table across from us: 'Well, Margaret, Zulma, I did some thinking and a little praying, not too much mind you, don't believe in overloading the circuits. I want to help you both. When I was about your age, Zulma, I ran away – Margaret here has heard it all, been bored by it no doubt.' She smiled at me. 'Things were different then, somewhat harder maybe, but then when I hear your story Zulma . . . you know, child, not much has changed, not much at all, and that makes me sad, real sad . . . we still know how to make each other's life a misery.

'Running away – sometimes it's the only thing you can do – and don't let nobody tell you different; sometimes it does help, sometimes you just have to run. I was thinking last night that maybe I'd give you girls the money, so you could get to Zulma's gran. I have quite a bit saved and no chick nor child to spend it on, except Mr Billings – and Lord, he's one big child.' She chuckled. 'Anyway, I figured that if I did that I'd be encouraging you to run, though neither of you need any encouragement from the looks of it. I don't know much about the law – not that I want to know more either, but it's a gut feeling I have – that it would be different from just buying the tickets for you with your mammy's money. But even that bothers me, I just don't like the idea of your mammy worrying about that money . . . not to say worrying about you!'

Neither me nor Zulma said anything. I was hoping that Mrs B would say what I wanted her to say, yet was afraid of hearing.

'See girls, I am caught good and proper; if I don't help you and you girls run off, as you say you are going to do, then I'm as much to blame. I hear things in what you say, Zulma, that take me back years and years. And Margaret, you only what –

thirteen, fourteen? But you right as anybody ever was to say children have no rights, and no power, and Lord help them if some adult take it in mind to abuse them – and abuse is not only physical abuse. They got no recourse, they got to take the law into their own hands sometimes. I suppose they could call the Children's Aid, but no child wants to turn in a parent . . . But I always say the Lord helps those who help themselves. There I go again talking too much – some more peach cobbler? Good, I like to see good food eaten with pleasure.' She dished out some more peach cobbler and ice cream.

'Now where was I? Oh yes, the Lord helps them who help themselves, so if I don't help you, I'm responsible; if I help you I'm also responsible. Seems to me that since I'm responsible anyhow, I should do what would make most people happy, with least danger to you two, and myself. I hate the police and courts and all that – Lord, I was so confused last night – seemed any which way I turned I was responsible. I even thought of talking to Mr Billings, and Lord knows, I have to be *very* confused to want to talk to him. Often he just confuses me more. Then I decided not to – most times, you know, you're better off with men not knowing your thoughts; they're contrary folk, men, very contrary. But you girls can't be expected to know what I mean, except that I'm responsible. So, to make a long story short – I'm going to help you.'

'Oh Mrs B, I knew you would, I just knew it.' I ran around the table and threw my arms around her, 'I told you so, Zulma, I told you so.'

'Hold on there, girlie, hold on! Not so fast, it's not so easy or simple. What I want to do is talk to your parents – both of you,' she said, looking at both of us.

I was so disappointed I could have cried. I knew it, I knew it – just like an adult – she was going to tell our parents about what we planned to do.

'I have to talk to them. Remember the word, responsible? Well, I wouldn't be responsible if I didn't talk to them – wait a second, Margaret, I know what you're going to say, but let me finish. I'm not going to tell them what you have told me, what your plans are, or even about the money. You took me in your confidence, and what both of you girls have told me stays with me, O.K.?'

I felt a little better, but not much.

'I want to see,' Mrs B continued, 'whether I can persuade them to let you girls do what you most want to do. Zulma, you want to go back to your Gran in Tobago – that will be a lot better for you, for your mother and your stepfather. Margaret, you want Zulma to go back to her Gran, because you know she'll be happier there. You want to stay here this summer and not go to your grandmother in Barbados. So tomorrow evening, I'm going to see everyone – Bertha Billings can be quite persuasive when she wants to be, and maybe, just maybe, there's an easier way out of this than you girls running away. Come on my girls, cheer up, don't look so down.'

'He won't agree, Mrs B, he won't,' I said to her. 'I know my father.'

Zulma shook her head, 'Me mum's not going to send me back, and even if she wanted to, he not going give she any money for de fare.'

'Wait. If they refuse – and what you kids are asking for seems quite reasonable to me – if they refuse, I promise you you've got my help. How's that? So Tuesday evening, right after school, you girls come on by here, and we'll see where things are at – you'll probably know by then anyway. Cheer up now, no poker faces.'

19

For the second time I was right, about my father, first with Mrs Chalmers, now with Mrs B. It was Tuesday evening and we were in Mrs B's kitchen waiting to hear what she had to say about meeting with our parents. Zulma and I each had a bowl of ice cream and a slice of home-made apple pie.

'I was right wasn't I Mrs B? My dad didn't agree for me to stay.'

Mrs B sighed and sat down at the table in the kitchen; she looked like she had bad news for us.

'Yes . . . look girls . . . I know parents are put down here to look after children; if God didn't intend for us to be guided by them, he wouldn't have given us parents, yes? But sometimes . . .' she sighed again. 'Your parents – both of you I mean – are . . . well difficult . . . especially the men. I don't quite know what to say without sounding like I'm criticising them . . . I know they believe they're doing the best for you, but they're beyond reasoning with; their best is final, absolute, and there's no reasoning with them; they don't intend to let anybody else get a word or suggestion in edgewise. And it's the men more so than your mothers, I must say.

'Your father Margaret, hmm hmm, hmm, – Cuthbert Cruickshank – hah, there's a man that wants control, of everything. He rules Tina, he has a son who does his every bidding, and Jo-Ann, well I've seen her in church enough times to know she hasn't got a serious thought in that pretty head of hers. You bother him, Margaret – he as much as said that to me – because he doesn't understand you, can't quite control your mind like the others; and he has to have control, so he'll control your body, your movements. I hate to say it, but that's how I see it.

'Your mother, God bless her, is useless as far as standing up to him. I know she's a good mother, but he never listens to her, and I could see she was on your side Margaret, in her own way . . . I don't think she understands you either, but she knows how badly you don't want to go, and I could see she wasn't happy about what your father's doing. I made them promise not to punish you for telling me anything – told them it was all my doing – coming to talk to them. At one point, you know, I said to Cuthbert: "D'you realise that children are running away every day from home for less reason than Margaret has, because they're misunderstood or unhappy?" He puffs up his chest like a pouter pigeon, and says to me: "I am West Indian, my daughter is West Indian, and she does as I say in my house. She goes where *I* tell her, and I'll have none of her womanish behaviour in my house." I said to him, "Cuthbert, I have known you for many years now; from what I hear you're one hell of a dominoes player, but you know nothing about raising children, and what I just heard you say is the biggest pile of fartiatic nonsense I have ever heard in all my sixty-five years. What do you think your daughter is, a horse? She's a human being, man – a half-grown one maybe – but that doesn't make her less of one." I thought he was going to have a fit, you could tell that no one ever tells Cuthbert Cruickshank he's talking nonsense. Well I did and I'm glad. But you were right, Margaret, I didn't get anywhere with him.

'Your parents, Zulma – now there's a horse of a different colour – or I should say a mule of a different colour, but still a mule. Your poor mother – how she ever hooked up with a man like that is beyond me. She's a fine woman, and gentle too, I could tell. Your stepfather? Now there's some very rough business, and unpleasant too. He barely looked up from the T.V. when I was there, except to say he had no money to waste on

113

you any more. If he could have spat at me, I'm sure he would have. Your mother was really embarrassed.

'You were right too, he has no intention of putting out any money for your fare. He said he paid for you to come here, and that was enough. I told your mother you were unhappy, couldn't learn anything as long as you were here, and that you were better off with your gran. She started to cry. He said you thought you were a big woman, and wanted to come between him and his wife; and that if you couldn't live there, they would find a foster-home for you. "But the child wants to go to her gran – why not send her – at least you would know she was happy", I said. "Her grandmother too old", was his reply, and I wanted to say, "and you're too stupid", but I held my tongue. He went on: "All she want do is turn she mother head with she own way. Once she back there, she going want fe come up to Canada again, and who going have fe pay for she – me one." Didn't you say your mother worked, Zulma? She must have some money of her own.'

'He take it all, Mrs Billings, she don't have nothing for she self.'

Mrs B shook her head and frowned: 'Women! Men! Why God ever thought it was a good idea, I don't know. Seems there's more problems in that arrangement than warrants the trouble.'

'So are you going to help us now Mrs B,' I said, 'now that they have said no?'

Mrs B still looked worried. I couldn't figure it out. The last time we saw her she said she would help us if our parents said no, and now she didn't look like she wanted to.

'Mrs B what's wrong – have you changed your mind about helping us?' I asked.

She sighed again. 'After your parents said no, I decided not to waste any time, so I made enquiries about tickets and all that . . . and I can't do it girls.'

'What d'you mean you can't do it Mrs B? Why can't you do it?' I asked.

'I have to have your parents' consent, at least one of them, to get the tickets and I don't,' Mrs B's face was heavy and sad, 'so I can't help you – not that way . . .'

'Damn blast and damn again!' I said before I realised what I was saying. 'I'm sorry Mrs B.'

'Sorry? For what? A few swear words – if it makes you feel better go right ahead – I know a few too, but they not going to help you girls right now, only make me feel better.'

We were all silent. I didn't dare look at Zulma but I knew how she must be feeling; I wondered if the band around her chest had come back. Everything had been a waste of time – I could see me going to Barbados, and Zulma running away, alone – somewhere awful . . . the ticking of the kitchen clock was loud.

'Unless . . . unless, yes – that's it!' I heard Mrs B say these words, but they didn't mean anything to me. 'C'mon girls, more apple pie, ice cream?' We refused. Why the hell was she so suddenly happy, didn't she understand what was facing us? I didn't say anything, just sat there.

'Listen now girls, I have another plan,' she stroked my cheek and Zulma's. 'I think I know how you feel, but trust me; I have one last thing I want to try before we give up hope completely. I'm not going to tell you what it is, but I have a hunch it just might work.' She came around the table to where we were both sitting and hugged us close. 'Come on, cheer up girls, trust Bertha. You're looking at one of the most accomplished runaways, yes?'

She got up and went to a calendar on the kitchen wall. 'All right, girls, let's see. Today is Tuesday, I want to see you both here on Sunday – about two in the afternoon – no later, o.k? It'll all work out, one way or the other; trust me, I just have a feeling and my feelings are usually right.' She wrapped up what was left of the apple pie in two separate parcels, and gave them to us as we were leaving.

Zulma and I didn't talk much on the way home, we just

couldn't, it was all up to Mrs B. But even if she couldn't help us we still had the money, and we could still run away – that thought made me feel better. I wish I knew what Mrs B had planned though.

20

Nothing in my life happens in halves. There was a time when nothing on my list had changed, now suddenly I had money enough to help Zulma, enough for me to run far away from HIM; and as if that wasn't enough, my period had to go and start.

Don't get me wrong – it wasn't that I wasn't happy – or relieved. It was proof, wasn't it, that I wasn't a freak – I was normal, but of all the times to go and start – now when I had all these things to worry about.

I was really cool about it though, you wouldn't think I had been wanting this to happen. It was like – so this is what it's all about eh? Almost a sort of let-down. My mum had a record by Peggy Lee that she used to play a lot sometimes – there was one song that always struck me – *Is That All There Is*, about this little girl looking at a fire for the first time and thinking, 'Is that all there is?' Then the girl grows up and falls in love and she asks the same question again, 'Is that all there is?' That was what I felt and thought when my period happened – is that all there is?

I don't know what I expected, but there I was lying on my bed reading on Friday evening and suddenly I feel this wetness. I thought for sure I had peed myself, so I ran to the bathroom and there it was, my blood. So I got my pads and put one on like my mum had shown me, and thought, 'Now what?' No boys must touch me now I thought, and smiled to myself.

I wanted to tell someone. I called Zulma and she wasn't home; Jo-Ann was out – probably sneaking off seeing old pimply-face when I had important things to tell her. That left my mother who wouldn't have been my first choice.

117

She was in the kitchen ironing; HE was watching T.V., asleep as usual.

'Hi Mum – what's going on?'

'Nothing much.'

I sat down and watched her pushing the iron back and forth, back and forth. She and I hadn't talked much since my 'deportation order', but I remembered what Mrs B had said about her being on my side. That made me feel better about her.

'Mum?'

'Hmmmm?'

'It's happened.'

'What's happened, Harr . . . I mean Margaret?'

'My period's happened – and I mustn't let any boys touch me right?' I smiled at her as I said this. She stopped ironing and looked at me, and this great, big humungous smile broke out over her face. She put her hands up to her face and laughed out loud – like a girl. I don't think I had ever heard my mother laugh like this – or if I had, it had been so long ago I had forgotten how nice it sounded and how . . . well, how nice and pretty she was.

'Oh Margaret, you're a young lady now!' She came round the ironing-board, and threw her arms around me.

'I'm not a lady Mum – I'm a woman. Ladies don't swear, remember?'

She laughed again. 'You're terrible Margaret. Back home in Jamaica, that's what we used to say when it happened – that you're a young lady.'

We both smelt it at the same time – the smell of something burning.

'Something's burning Mum!'

'Hell, your father's shirt!' She held up a white shirt with a huge brown burn in the back. I wanted to say 'great', but didn't.

'Is one of his favourite ones too. I'll just say it lose.'

'Tell him you burnt it – maybe he'll start ironing his own – right Mum?' We both started laughing again.

118

'Margaret!' she was trying hard to be serious, but she couldn't do it; she started to laugh again.

'If is one thing I hate, is ironing. It would be a great way of getting out of it.'

We were both giggling – I had never seen my mum quite like this before – like she was a little drunk. 'I should have a period every day,' I thought; then I realised it was going to be often enough, every month, no point in overdoing a good thing.

My mum was banging the iron around. 'I hate housework, you know, I figure I do enough in one lifetime.'

'So why do it? I won't ever ever do it when I'm living on my own.'

'Huh, that's youth talking. Wait till you're married and have children and a husband, you going have to do it.'

'No way Mum – no way – no housework for me – except for myself, sometimes. And only what I *have* to do. I will never iron a man's shirt, never.' My mum laughed again, but it wasn't a real happy laugh.

'You're a woman now Margaret. There are some things you going have to do – to put up with. Hear me, I know what I saying; now is your period, then there's childbirth . . . just wait till the pain of childbirth lick you, you don't feel nothing till you feel that. Then there's housework and grocery shopping and trying to keep your husband happy – is not easy, Margaret, but is best if you face up to it now and don't expect differently – it will make it a lot easier for you to bear.'

'No Mum, you're wrong I *am* going to make it different. I won't get married, I won't have babies, and I won't iron any man's shirt – specially if I don't like ironing.'

My mum looked at me over the ironing-board – seemed like it was for a long time. She wasn't laughing any more, and her eyes were real bright and shiny; I could see the tears in them.

'Oh Margaret, Margaret, you setting yourself up for trouble. I don't want to see you hurt, you expect too much, too much, child.' Her 'child' was like Mrs B's – it made me feel warm and

119

protected, but I knew she was wrong – you didn't have to put up with anything if you didn't want to.

I went over to her and kissed her cheek. 'Night Mum. I won't let any boys touch me, right?' We laughed again, this time her laugh was a little happier. 'By the way, Mum, where mustn't I let the boys touch me, you haven't ever told me?'

She slapped me on the bum, 'Go on with you and stop teasing.' She laughed again.

21

I don't know what I was expecting when we got to Mrs B, but Zulma and I were hoping she had a small miracle for us. My grandmother was visiting New York, but in two or three weeks she was going to be back in Barbados. Sometime after that I was going to be leaving. I couldn't get a set date from my mum, which made me even more anxious.

When we had finished our corn pone and milk, Mrs B asked us to go to the basement rec. room and watch T.V. until she called us. An hour later she came down to get us, all smiles.

'Come on girls, come on – do I have a surprise for you both.' Zulma and I looked at each other, shrugged and followed her.

Whatever it was that I was expecting it wasn't my mum or Zulma's mum, but there they were, both of them sitting in Mrs B's kitchen, both of them smiling. Surprised? Yes – I was. Worried? Yes, I still was. So I didn't say much, or anything. I waited to hear what they had to say.

When Zulma had come into the room, Mrs Clarke, her mum, had got up and gone over and hugged her. I could tell Zulma was really surprised.

My mum looked at me and smiled. 'Hello Margaret,' was all she said. Since our kitchen conversation I felt closer to her, but she was an adult and I didn't, with the exception of Mrs B, trust adults much.

I looked at Mrs B. 'Well girls,' she said, 'you probably didn't expect this surprise; but I told you I would work it out, and I have.' I was still looking at Mrs B – she could tell I didn't understand what she meant.

'Well, let me start at the beginning. When I saw you girls last, you remember how down we all were. Your parents were not going to budge an inch – at least your fathers – ' She looked at my mum and Zulma's and smiled. 'I couldn't get tickets for you without your parents' permission. What kept bothering me was that it was the men who were being difficult, Cuthbert, and your stepfather, Zulma. I just had a hunch that if I could talk to your mothers alone, I could make them see sense. It was a risk, I know, but I felt that if I could only show them that both of you were pretty desperate, and were going to run away, then their love for you was going to be more important than being right – or exercising power over you.

'I had to convince them that you were serious. The only way to do that was to tell them about the money – that you had the money, that you knew it was wrong to keep it, but that you were both set on keeping it and using it to help yourselves out of difficult situations – no, impossible situations. If your mammies were to know this, I knew it would move them. I also knew I had to get them away from the men; I knew I could make them see sense – how unhappy you both were.

'I also knew that if my hunch didn't prove right, I was going to help you both – in any way I could, short of breaking the law – and I told your mammies as much. So I did, I took a risk and told them both. I met with each of them separately, alone, and explained the situation; we agreed to meet here again today, and here we are.

'Margaret, I told your mammy what I thought Cuthbert was trying to do to you, break your spirit; but I'm not going to talk for her. Tina, your turn.'

My mum looked at me and smiled again. She spoke slowly: 'Margaret I know I haven't defended you enough with your dad. He's a difficult man to live with, I should know . . .'

Mrs B butted in; '. . . You sure right about that, Tina, you deserve a medal.'

My mum smiled and sighed: 'You probably right, Bertha, but I made my choice, and he is a good man in a lot of ways.'

'You sure did, Tina – and what a choice, but go on – don't let me interrupt you. I've seen worse, a lot worse.'

'It was your getting your period that did it Margaret.' She could tell I didn't understand.

'I would probably have agreed with Bertha and done what I'm doing now. I don't know if I would have felt as right as I do now though. I was so happy for you when you told me about being a young woman – not lady right?' She smiled at me. 'It make me realise that you growing up Margaret, you not my baby any more. I want to see you grow up. I don't know how long your father was intending to leave you with his mother, but even a year is too long. I know you different from Jo-Ann, I understand her better, and I do wish you would wear dresses and be more like a girl, but you is my daughter just like Jo-Ann – my baby – and I don't want no one, not even Cuthbert, sending you away for a long time.

'When you told me about getting your period . . .' she stopped talking and like she was going to cry, but she took a deep breath, and continued. '. . . I don't know what to say . . . except that I don't want to lose you . . . You know I felt so bad when Bertha talked to me after that; here you had to go to another woman for help with your own mother still alive . . . that hurt, because there was many a day when I wished for my mother to be alive to help me, and here my own daughter couldn't come to me for help. Oh that hurt Bertha, I not blaming you, just myself, just myself.'

'Well, you should stop that right now, Tina,' said Mrs B. 'Children are not all the same, and Margaret here is a bright one. She would challenge anybody, you just have to handle her different, and contrary to what Cuthbert thinks, this is not the West Indies – it's Canada, it's the eighties and growing up was never an easy thing to do.'

I couldn't believe my ears – *my* mother had been saying these things – she who never used to stick up for me. You could have pushed me over with your little finger.

Then Zulma's mother started talking and crying. She was a round, soft, brown woman – all different shades of brown – her eyes, her hair, her skin; Zulma said her nickname used to be Sapodilla, like the fruit, because she was so brown. She said she was sorry that Zulma and her stepfather didn't get along, that she had been waiting a long time for Zulma to come to Canada and live with her, and how much she used to miss Zulma when she first came up to Canada. There was many a night, she said, she used to cry herself to sleep, missing her, but she held out because she was trying to make a better life for her, Zulma, herself and her mum – Gran; but that Gran had told her a long time ago that she wasn't interested in 'big country', she liked her island and she wasn't going anywhere. After all the years of struggle, she was finally able to bring Zulma up, but it just wasn't working out like she wanted it to, and she knew it wasn't Zulma's fault.

Zulma began to cry too.

'But Zulma,' her mum continued, 'is always your happiness I wanted, and if you want to go back to Gran, you should go. I going miss you, and I know Gran going say I should never have send for you, but I had to; that was why I was in Canada, to make a better life for you. I have some money save your stepfather don't know about.' Now that was a real shock to Zulma, I bet; she had always thought her stepfather took all her mother's money. 'I'll buy your ticket. What he going do, carry on for a while?'

'What if he hit you again?' Zulma asked.

Zulma's mum dropped her head. 'I don't think so,' she said, 'I tell him, after the last time, if he so much as lay a finger on me again, I going leave him, and I mean it.' She and Zulma looked at each other.

Then my mum said to Zulma's mum, 'I want to help, Carol. Margaret has been asking me for months to help Zulma, and I used to say it wasn't my business but it is, and I want to help. You know sometimes I wonder whether is the cold that make us so closed-in and narrow in this country, only concentrating on your own life. Years ago, I didn't think anything about bringing this old white lady into my home and helping her; I couldn't bear to see her so lonely, and that was what people was for, to help each other. Yet somehow I just turned a deaf ear when Margaret kept telling me how unhappy Zulma was. I don't know whether it was because they was children, but I should know better; I know trouble is no respecter of age . . .'

Mrs B interrrupted again: '. . . Tina let's just say thank God we found out in time to help, before they did something foolish. Thank God you have a daughter like Margaret who had the brains enough to come and talk to someone, some kids might have just run. You know at that age they think seven-hundred dollars could last them a lifetime – you should be proud, both of you, of these girls.'

'Thanks Bertha, thanks for saying that . . . I would feel better about everything if the girls were to use the money that Margaret found for their fares. I was going to buy a water-bed for me and Cuthbert, and modelling lessons for Jo-Ann.'

'You're right Tina, the last thing Jo-Ann needs is modelling lessons, she needs a little more seriousness in her life right now; and as for your water-bed – well I don't want to comment, but aren't you and Cuthbert a little old for all that hippie stuff – next you going to be telling me that you and he going to be getting high together.' Mrs B and my mum laughed.

'That'll be the day,' my mum said, 'when Cuthbert gets high.' She laughed again.

'Mum!' I had to shout to make myself heard, she and Mrs B were having a grand old time. 'Mum, what do you mean by fares, I thought I wasn't going to Barbados?'

'You're not.'

'Well where are you sending me – you said fares?'

'I did. I'm sending you to Zulma's gran for the summer, if that's O.K. with you. It's O.K. with Zulma's gran, Carol here checked already.'

'Holy Holy Shiiit! Tobago! Me and Zulma? Oh hell, this is too much!' I saw my mother's face register the swear words –

'I'm sorry Mum, I just had to, and Mrs B says it's O.K. sometimes if it makes you feel better.'

My mother wasn't amused: 'I thought the news of your going to Tobago would be enough to make you feel better. I don't see how bad words could make you feel better, and I'm sure Mrs Billings didn't say that.'

'That's all right Tina, I can defend myself – I did say something like that. I never think of words being good or bad, Tina. In the mouths of some people the word God can be a profanity; I just think it's the occasion that makes them acceptable or not.'

'What about Dad?' I asked.

She shrugged. 'What's he going to do Margaret, rant and rave and go on about me going behind his back, but he's not going to divorce me, is he?'

'More's the pity,' Mrs B said. My mum laughed.

'Come on Bertha, they do have their uses now, don't they?' It was Mrs B's turn to laugh.

'Truly spoken, Tina, truly spoken. I think we may be giving these girls a wrong impression about men, I hope they don't believe that all men are controlling or beating their wives. Mr Billings now is a gem, quite a gem.'

'Yes, you're lucky Bertha. But to get back to your father Margaret, when I tell him that you had made plans to run away, that is bound to affect him; he doesn't think anybody will ever go against him – you're the first Margaret. He'll have all summer to cool down in any case, and he's just going to have to accept that I want to live with my daughters, both of them – I might even teach them how to iron shirts, right?' She smiled at me.

'No way, Mum. Maybe I'll teach you how to burn a few more.' She laughed. 'You know what, Mum . . . ?'

'No, what?'

'You are real cool – ab-so-lute, just ab-so-lute. Every one should have mums like you and Mrs Clarke.' I turned to Mrs B. 'How did you know they would agree Mrs B?'

Mrs B smiled and looked around the room – at all of us. 'Well at the risk of stating the obvious and being accused of being partial, we're all women aren't we?' We all laughed. 'Come on now, some more corn pone for everyone – and milk for you girls.'

For the next hour the planning went on. Mrs Clarke agreed to let my mum pay for the tickets, that way there would be one less thing for Zulma's mum to have to explain, and one less thing for Zulma's stepfather to have to get angry about. Mrs B also thought that Mrs Clarke should hang on to that money: 'You never know,' she said, 'you may be needing it for yourself one day.'

Zulma's mum and my mum agreed that if Zulma wanted to come up again some time in the future, and her mum was still living with her stepfather, Zulma could come and live with us. That was just fantastic – just fantastic. I reached out and took Zulma's hand; we looked at each other and smiled.

'Remember,' I said, 'I promised you.'

She nodded. 'Me know, me know, but me did do some praying too.' We both laughed.

I got a real charge out of HIM not being involved in my going, and knowing that he thought I was going to Barbados. I wished I could see his face when my mum told him – oh how I wished I could.

I knew my mum was going to be O.K. if she could defy my dad in this way, and over me too. She was more than O.K., she was ab-so-lute. Zulma's mum too – both of them, the three of them, Mrs B too – real cool ladies – I mean women, ab-so-lute women. Little did I know how soon my mum would be called upon to show how ab-so-lute she really was.

22

After we women made our plans, everything went real quickly
– new clothes, tickets, passports; my mum didn't tell my dad a
thing. She let him think I was on my way to Barbados. She now
had an extra something in her voice when she spoke to him –
like the days of taking crap from him were coming to an end –
and fast. You could tell he didn't like her tone sometimes, or her
answering him back sharply, or insisting she was right about
something. I just hoped my mum could keep it up, and not let
him get her down.

One of the things I had to do before I left was update my LIST
OF THINGS I WANT CHANGED IN MY LIFE. My father was not going
to be a problem to me, at least not for the next two months: He
was getting his wish; I was going to get some 'Good West
Indian Discipline', but not from where he expected.

It was funny though, funny strange, not funny ha ha, that
there were times when I felt sort of sorry for him, and just a little
bit sad that I was not going to see him for a while.

One evening I was in the living room, he was reading the
newspapers as usual. I hadn't realised I was staring at him,
until he told me it was rude to stare and asked if I didn't have
anything to do.

'No Dad, I just want to sit here with you.'

He gave me this sharp look, and held up the newspaper in
front of his face again.

'Tell me about Barbados,' I said. He peered at me over his
newspaper.

'Now?'

'Yes, now. Tell me about all the things you used to do and how you liked playing cricket.'

'Margaret, I want to read the newspaper, *now*. Can't you find a better time to ask me about Barbados? Besides, you're going to find out all about it in a few weeks' time.'

'I want you to talk to me now,' I said.

'No, I'm busy. If you're bored, I can find something for you to do.' I got up and left, feeling mad and sad at the same time – I just wish, I thought, he could see me, and like me and be nice to me.

When I told Zulma about this, she laughed and said that now she was leaving, she could actually see what her mother liked in her stepfather, that he was real funny sometimes. But I was still glad I was going to be away from my dad for a while – and so was she, about her stepfather.

Now that Zulma was leaving, she and her mum had got real close; she was worried her stepfather might beat up her mum when he found out what she'd done in sending her back to her gran. Mrs B had said that she would be there when Zulma's mum told her stepfather, and that she would take all the responsibility for it. She also said she would keep a real 'high profile', and if he so much as laid a finger on her mum, her mum was to call her. If Zulma's mum wanted to leave, she could come and stay with her, Mrs B – she had lots and lots of room, she said, especially for Zulma's mum.

Next on my list – my mother's attitude. What could I say? She liked me and wanted me around. That much I now knew. She was still bugging me to straighten my hair, and wear skirts – I guess she wouldn't be my mum if she didn't do these things – she wasn't dead yet, right? But she was great.

And Zulma (back to my list again), well I had kept my promise, hadn't I, with a 'little help from my friends' of course, and she was going back to her gran.

I had given up on the things that weren't so important, or those I couldn't change – my sister's weight, my brother's pimples, my breasts, which still seemed really small.

129

My period had happened, so all in all it wasn't a bad score at all for someone who started out with a whole heap of things she wanted changed.

There was still the problem of my name, of course. There was no way HE would let me change it legally to Harriet and I wasn't so sure any more if I wanted to change it to Harriet. I mean I had done something as Margaret, hadn't I? – the Underground Railroad Game, and getting Zulma back to her gran, indirectly – so now Margaret meant something, right? Well it did, to me, at least. I was also thinking that if I was going to change my name, I might like an African name, something really different and special, and I knew HE would have a fit. A daughter with an African name – I would have to do a lot of convincing, so that would probably have to wait until I was adult. Margaret, Harriet, both names meant something to me now, and I wasn't going to worry about names for the next little while.

I was going to miss Jo-Ann though – surprise of surprises – my old Slobbo, Chub Queen of a sister. With my hard-earned cash, my Zulma savings, I went out and bought her the biggest, ugliest, most humungous pair of earrings. They were bound to touch her shoulders, and I knew she would love them. Dear Jo, I wrote in my goodbye note (my mum said she would give it to her after I left), I do love you. I don't always like you though. I'll miss your fat ha! ha! Hope you like your earrings; you'd better, since I spent *all* – well almost all – my money on them. I hope they're big enough and I'll write you from Tobago. P.S. Have you ever thought of wearing a nose ring – these earrings would look great as nose rings – they would cover your mouth and you wouldn't eat as much and you would lose weight, right? Your ever loving sister, Margaret/Harriet. P.P.S. You're not really fat and even if you were it wouldn't matter – it's who you are that counts. To be really, really honest I wish I had a few curves like you – if you *ever* use this against me I'll kill you – I promise!!

In a short note to my brother, I wished him luck in his

130

elections as Rib Roast Prime Minister; I couldn't think of anything else to say to him, we never talked.

I thought of writing my dad, I even made a few starts, but I couldn't get anywhere. I would either get real mad with him for not liking me enough, or get real sad and hurt about him sending me away so easily. I tore up a lot of paper and swore a lot – maybe, I thought, when I get to Tobago I'll be able to write to him – maybe.

23

All the while I was getting myself ready to leave, a little voice at the back of my head kept telling me that this was too good to be true – me and Zulma going away together, my mother helping me . . . I didn't want to think it, but every so often the thought would pop into my mind, a horrible thought, that HE would find out about what we were doing. When it did happen, I had this feeling that I had been expecting it all along.

It was a Sunday – about four or five o'clock in the afternoon; my father had already had his sleep and was reading the newspaper in the living room. I was upstairs in my room lying across the bed reading a detective story by Agatha Christie, when I heard the doorbell ring; neither my sister nor my brother was at home so I groaned, rolled over and waited to see whether my mum or dad would answer. The bell went again. Hell, I thought, my mum was probably somewhere where she couldn't hear it, and of course HE would never interrupt his reading to do something so ordinary like answer the doorbell. The bell went again, 'I'm coming,' I yelled, and ran downstairs making as much noise as possible to disturb him – my father liked the house to be quiet on a Sunday and this was my way of getting at him for not going to answer the door.

I opened the door and felt myself go all funny. My legs felt like they were going to collapse and my underarms were suddenly wet.

'Your father home?'

Mr Clarke, Zulma's stepfather, was standing there. He had

never come to our house before, and one look at his face told me everything.

I opened my mouth to answer him but I couldn't say anything, I just nodded and turned away to go and get my father. I didn't go right into the living room but stood close to the door.

'Dad.' He still held the newspaper up to his face. 'Dad!' I said more loudly. 'Dad, Mr Clarke is here to see you.' He looked up surprised.

'Mr Clarke?'

'Zulma's stepfather.'

'Well show him in then – don't just stand there.'

I didn't need to – without my knowing it Mr Clarke had followed me, and when I turned around to get him, he was standing right behind me. I jumped and made a noise almost like a little scream but I caught myself in time. I hate girls like my sister who scream and ooh and aah, but I *was* surprised and I was also scared – really scared – about what was going to happen. Mr Clarke brushed past me and walked into the room.

'A very good day to you, sir,' he said.

My father got up and made to shake hands with him; Mr Clarke ignored his outstretched hand: 'I don't like bother a man in his house on a Sunday, but there is something I must talk to you about, sir.'

'Please, have a seat, have a seat.' My father waved him to a chair and at the same time made a gesture with his arm shooing me outside.

I left quickly, pulling the door behind me but not closing it completely. I didn't even think about it; I was going to listen. I stood right behind the door and strained my ears to hear what they were saying.

It was bad, real bad. Mr Clarke had found out that Mrs Clarke and my mother were sending Zulma and me to her gran in Tobago. I noticed that I was so tense and trying so hard to hear that I was holding my breath – I had to tell myself to breathe. He didn't tell my father how he had found out and I

133

would have bet all the money I had found that he had gone snooping. I felt my stomach cramping hard with worry for Zulma and her mother – what had he done when he found out . . . ? I could feel the sweat trickling down my body, and heard Mr Clarke's voice rising while my father did his reasonable act, trying to calm him.

'Is this country I tell you, sir, it full up they head with all this feminist talk and make them feel woman is boss. Every day you turn on the T.V. is somebody else talking about how women have to have they rights; they want to wear pants and run man life, and time and time again I have to tell my wife that two man-rat can't live in one hole.'

I strained to hear what my father had to say to that; I knew he believed what Mr Clarke had just said only he would never put it that crudely. He would talk about discipline, and how 'there has to be one head to any organisation for it to function well'. I had heard him enough times on this subject before. I couldn't hear what he said, his voice was only a low murmur, then I heard Mr Clarke again:

'Woman have to know their place, don't it sir?'

'Yes, yes, well thank you Mr Clarke for telling me about this – I'll look into it. I'm sure you must be mistaken, but I will talk to my wife about it.'

I ran around the corner and up the stairs before they came out.

'Tina! Tina!' I heard my father calling my mother.

I crept down the stairs just in time to see her coming out of the kitchen – she must have been in the basement. If only she had heard the doorbell and answered it, I thought, she could have prevented Mr Clarke from coming in. I had a quick image of my mother slamming the door in his face. But thoughts like these were a waste of time: my father now knew about our plans and I was going nowhere fast. He was going to do his old 'I know best, Tina' routine, and now that he had caught her out hiding the truth from him, she didn't even have a leg to stand on.

My mum saw me on the stairs and I drew a line across my neck to tell her that we had had it. She raised her eyebrows in surprise; I shrugged to show that I didn't quite know what was going on. She went into the living room.

'Close the door, Tina.' I crept down the stairs and was now just outside the living room once again; I was sure my mother knew this because when she pushed the door shut, she didn't close it completely. I was bolder this time and sat on the floor just outside the door, pulling my knees up to my chin and wrapping my arms around them. I was holding myself tight – very tight – I felt safer that way . . . in a small tight ball. It felt good to have a wall against my back, I was feeling a little dizzy. There were so many thoughts spinning around my head – we were so close to escaping . . . now I would have to go to Barbados like he wanted all along. My mind leapt from that to Zulma . . . she would be sent to a foster-home. I would never see her again.

'What's this I hear about Margaret going to Tobago?' my father's voice cut across this last thought. 'She is going to Barbados to my mother, is she not?'

'No, she's not.' Just like that, I couldn't believe my ears – my mother didn't even bother to ask who he had heard it from, it was like she didn't even care, and her voice was hard and tight like I had never heard it before. All those times when she hadn't stood up for me, and had let him push her around, were wiped out with those three words: 'No, she's not'.

'What do you mean "she's not"?'

'You heard me, Cuthbert, she's not. She not going because I'm sending her to Zulma's grandmother in Tobago for the summer, and then she coming back here – to live with us, her family – like she ought to.'

I buried my face in my knees; my underarms were wet, my T-shirt soaked. I don't know if I was more worried about Zulma and her mother or my mother and me – I had never heard that rough, hard tone in her voice before.

135

'But Tina, you and I decided she would be going to my mother in Barbados, didn't we?'

'No, Cuthbert, *we* didn't decide, *you* decided, like you decide everything in this house. And you know I wasn't in agreement with it from the beginning. She is my daughter, Cuthbert, as much as she is yours, and I have as much right as you do to decide what happen to her, and we been too hard on her – much too hard. Is not fair,' my mother's voice sounded like she was crying, 'is not fair; she is my last girl-child and already she going to other people for help – as if she don't have no mother – I not dead yet, Cuthbert, and as long as I alive and have breath in my body and strength in my arms, I don't want no girl-child of mine have to turn to somebody else – no matter how kind they is – for help.'

'Who did she go to?'

'Mrs Billings – bless her soul.'

'She's a meddling old fool, Tina, and that child needs discipline.'

'She need love too, Cuthbert, *and* understanding. All the discipline in the world not going do her any good if she don't have love. I know she different from the other two – you don't have to tell me that – is there plain as the nose on your face, and God knows sometimes I wish I understand her more, but she is my flesh and blood too and I not giving up on her, or giving her up to someone else to mind. I want her here, with me, not off in the West Indies somewhere with your mother; besides times changing and . . .'

'Tina, listen to yourself. If anyone were to hear you talking they would think that sending a child home to the West Indies to grandparents is something so strange: it's part of our culture.'

'Listen to yourself for a change, Cuthbert. Is since when you care about this thing you calling West Indian culture? The only culture you value is the one you come and meet in this country. I watch you all these years putting down the West Indies and anything that come from there – this same culture you now

136

talking about. You turn up your nose at reggae, calypso and Caribana and anything that come from where we come from. If you could do without eating rice and peas and stew chicken, and salt fish and coocoo, you wouldn't eat any of that kind of food either. You want put yourself as far away from anything which mark you out as different from this culture. Cuthbert, this is a hard thing to say to you – is twenty-five years I living with you, but if you could change your skin I think you would.'

'You're talking a lot of nonsense, woman. Because I want the best for my children and my family, because I know . . .'

My mother didn't let him finish – she raised her voice above his which was already loud and angry: 'You let me talk Cuthbert Cruickshank.' I couldn't believe this was my mother – she who would let my father go on and on. 'You let me talk. I sick and tired of listening to you carry on about what *you* know – there's a lot you don't know and is time you wake up to that. For years you harass me about my partners' saving scheme and how it primitive and backward while you go off and play your damn foolish dominoes which you still shame about, and all the time you thinking you better than all the men you play with, because they haven't dropped what *you* call they backward ways. So since when West Indian culture – to use your words – so important to you?'

I think my father was as shocked as I was at my mother taking him on, and although I was glad that she was standing up for herself and for me, I was also really upset, too upset to enjoy my father getting what he had had coming to him for a long time. My mother continued:

'Is only because you don't know how to deal with the child why you want to send her away. Is what she do you why you so hard on her?'

'Tina, you know I only have her interests at heart.'

'You don't act that way, Cuthbert; you just down on her all the time. Is what more you want from her? She doing well in school and she not in trouble, she not involved with boys – you know how many girls her age have boyfriend already and know what sex is all about? So she faysty and have a mouth on her, but she need it in this world, because it rough out there, specially when you our colour. She just have to learn when to use it.'

I was crying and couldn't stop myself. Tears were coming from every opening, my nose, my eyes, my mouth, my pores . . . I hated people who slobbered, but that's what I was doing and I couldn't stop myself. I used my T-shirt to wipe my face and held the back of my left hand up to my mouth, biting on it hard to stop myself from making any noise. I wanted to stop them, to tell them they were grown-ups and were supposed to know better instead of them going on at each other like this. I had always known that most adults were con-artists who didn't run their lives any better than most kids – they just had more power – and here were my parents proving it to me. I could feel the anger and rage through the closed door and they weren't finished and I couldn't leave.

'Cuthbert, when I was Margaret age, I didn't have no mother to go to. I had to be everything to myself: mother, father, brother and sister. When I first start my monthlies is I one had to figure out what to do . . . you know what that feel like, Cuthbert?' My father was silent.

'I telling you now Cuthbert, you not sending my girl child nowhere to finish grow: not to your mother, or anybody mother, not even the Queen of England. I is her mother and I going stay that way. She going to Zulma grandmother for the summer – I think she need a break from all this – then she coming back here, and I know you don't like it but you just going to have to adjust yourself to it.'

'But you lied to me, Tina, right here in my own house.'

'Don't give me any of that "in my own house" talk, Cuthbert. Is my house too or you forget that, and don't try and change the subject. I didn't lie to you, I just didn't tell you. You believe she was going to your mother and I didn't tell you differently, and I don't feel good about doing it that way, but you didn't allow me

138

no other way because you too pigheaded to listen to anybody else.'

'When did you intend to tell me?'

'When I was good and ready.' My mother's words came slow and heavy like she was hammering something home.

'In other words, when she was gone.'

'That's right, Cuthbert.'

There was only a long silence from my father. I would have given anything to see his face. Was he running his hands over his balding head? He sometimes did this when he was thinking. Then I heard him clear his throat in that horrible way of his, as if he was about to say something, but my mother spoke up:

'Cuthbert, I have a lot of work to do – is there anything else you want right now?'

I thought I heard him say, 'No Tina, that'll be all,' but it was so low I could have imagined it.

I wiped my face again and went and sat on the stairs. My mother came out, stood at the living room door and looked over at me, her face heavy and sad with all that had gone on in the living room; I could tell she knew I had been listening. She made a gesture with her head for me to follow her to the kitchen.

In the kitchen she held me fiercely to her: I could smell her smell, warm and a little tangy with sweat and mixed with the Johnson's Baby Powder she always used. I held on to her like I never had before, never dared to. I was always too proud to show that I needed her and was hurt by her not understanding me, but now, for this little time in the kitchen, I could show that I needed her. And it felt so good, me and my mother standing there with all that love and pain between us . . . my mother and me . . . me and my mum . . . so different, yet so same, somehow. Why? Because we were women? I don't know, but I felt I understood her and her putting up with my father, *and* Mrs Clarke and her husband too. I would never live like them, I knew that, but Mum's standing up for me and my difference set something free in me to understand them and not judge them.

I pulled away suddenly, 'Mum, it was Mr Clarke who told Dad. Let's call Zulma and see what happened.'

'You right, Margaret.' I quickly dialled Zulma's number on the kitchen phone, but there was no answer.

'No answer Mum.'

'Try Mrs Billings.'

'Hello, Mrs B, this is Margaret, have you heard from Zulma? . . . Oh, she's there? Mrs B. our dads know. What?' I listened for a while, 'Oh no – yes, we'll come around. O.K.'

'Mum, both Zulma and her mum are there. I think something bad has happened; Mrs B wants us to come over.'

'I can't go now Margaret, I have to get your father's supper; I have a pretty good idea what happened, but you go and tell Mrs Billings I'll be over later in the evening.'

'Why don't you leave the meal – let *him* get it for himself?'

My mother smiled. 'That's a great idea, Margaret, but no. Your father get a great shock today. Apart from you, and he always had power over you because you're a child, no one ever stand up to him or go against him. It had to happen sometime and I blame myself for letting him get his own way for so long, and not putting up more of a fight – it seemed easier somehow . . . just to go along. I know things rough and ugly now, but it's all for the good, and is you we have to thank for it, for refusing to put up with what was wrong. But we can't make him feel like he lose all dignity . . . you know what I mean?'

I shook my head.

She pulled me close again, sat down and looked right into my eyes: 'We have to allow people their dignity and self-respect Margaret, even when we think they're wrong.'

'I just don't see why his dignity and self-respect depend on your cooking supper for him. I don't understand that, Mum.'

She laughed. 'You're right. It don't, but after what your father have to deal with today, it would be wrong to tell him to fix his own meal when I been doing it for over twenty years – that would be like throwing salt in his wounds.' She smiled,

'Who knows, there might come a time when he will fix a meal for all of us, but we have to take things step by step.

'He won't stop you going to Tobago and that is what is important right now. Let's leave the rest of the fight to me; I know Cuthbert Cruickshank only too well, so go on – go to Mrs Billings and find out what happened.'

If I had known what Mr Clarke had done before he had come to our house, I would have attacked him – kicked him where it would have hurt most. I know that sounds horrible, but when I saw Mrs Clarke's face I wanted to throw up. Mr Clarke had punched her in the eye, split her top lip; her face was a mess, and for the second time that day I began to cry. It was all I could do when I looked at Mrs Clarke's swollen face, one eye almost completely closed, across Mrs Billings' kitchen table.

Zulma filled me in on what had happened. She and her mother were going to church and Mr Clarke was giving them a ride. On the way there Mrs Clarke had asked him to mail a letter for her. She had forgotten to do it for the last two days and it was important that Gran get it as soon as possible.

'Me say he lower than low, Margaret – he can crawl under a razor blade with no problem – imagine he open me mother letter and read it, and of course he didn't like what he read there. When me and me mother get back home all hell break loose – is then ole mass start. He tell me mother she better explain what she mean in de letter – from what he say it look like me mother criticise him in de letter and say how he lay hand 'pon she. But is when he ask me mother to explain what she mean by when Gran see me, I will tell she everything, and she tell him I going home that he gone crazy. He start punching she in the face, in she side, and she crying and backing off from he, saying I'se she daughter and she only want the best for me, and me not happy here, and "please, Frank, no, please". I start screaming and try to get in between dem. He slap me a couple times and push me away, and he holding on to me mother by she wrist and pulling she towards he, so me take up a glass pitcher me mother have and break it over he hand, and is so he let she go – that is how I get me mother down de stairs and outside.' I remembered that Mr Clarke's hand had been bandaged when he came to our house.

Zulma continued: 'Me run next door and call de police. Dey come and go upstairs to talk to he, den dey talk to me mother who was waiting all dis time on de front porch. She say she was too shame to go to de neighbours – she didn't even want me to call de police. She say we family never mix up with police, and that is true, Margaret, Gran self tell me so, but there wasn't nothing else me could do. Anyway the police talk to me mother and ask she if she want to press charges. Quick, quick, me say, "Yes, she does", but she shake she head, so de police tell me to be quiet while dey talk to she. Me thought de police could charge he whether or not she want to press charges, Margaret.'

'I thought so too, but tell me what happened next.'

'Well, me say me was a witness, but me mother still shaking she head, so de police say dey warn he and dat if she decide to lay charges she should go and see somebody call a Justice of de Peace. Can you believe it, Margaret, before dey throw he in jail and throw way de key, dey give she a chance to think about it and a card with a name and de number of de police station to call if she want to talk to someone.' Zulma's voice was full of scorn for the police, and I agreed with her that they hadn't done enough to Mr Clarke; I thought jail was too good for him.

'After de police leave we decide to come over here to Mrs B; she take we to de hospital and de doctors dress me mother face – dey say she have a couple of bruise ribs too.' Zulma made a fist with one hand and pounded it in the open palm of her other hand. 'Boy, me would like to get me hands on he.'

Zulma told me all this down in Mrs B's basement where we were both sitting cross-legged on the carpeted floor. I told her what had happened at my place and then we were both quiet for a while.

'Margaret?'

'Hmmm.'

'You ever think that it real hard being a woman?'

142

'That's what I was thinking too, Zulma – your mum, my mum. I don't want to be like them; they have to put up with so much, and give so much, always thinking about someone else.'

'But you know when me think 'bout Gran, me don't feel that. Is like she live she life according to she own rules, and she not bending she life to fit into anybody else life – specially a man.'

'Maybe it's because she's old. Mrs B's different too.'

'What about Harriet, Margaret?'

'What about her?'

'You think she let men push she around?'

'Well she didn't let any white men, slave-owners I mean, push her around unless it was part of her plan. I don't ever want to depend on a man – ever, ever. They just take advantage of you.'

'Me too.'

'What's your mum going to do?'

Zulma shrugged. 'Maybe she will stay with Mrs B – that's what me would like she to do and that's what me been telling she she should do.'

We were quiet again – I reached out and took Zulma's hand and squeezed it hard; I did it as much for myself as for her. I wanted to tell her and myself that we had each other, our friendship, and that things would get better for us. We sat holding hands for a while.

'Margaret?'

'Yes.'

'You notice how we have to tell we mothers what is better for dem. Is almost like we is the mother and dey de children.'

I thought about what Zulma had said and nodded. It was true. There was a shift, ever so slight, between me and my mother. I don't know whether it was a shift in power. Maybe we understood each other better now than before. Maybe it was because we were both women. I sighed.

'You mustn't sigh too much you know, Margaret.'

'Why?'

'Gran say every time you sigh you lose an ounce of blood.'

143

I laughed, 'I don't know, Zulma, it's all so complicated that sometimes sighing is the only thing I can do.' I reached out for a piece of carrot cake and one of the glasses of milk on the tray between us. Mrs B never forgot to feed us. 'But I am glad I'm leaving for a while. My mum and dad are going to be having lots of arguments – I just know it – and I don't want to be around. I feel upset for both of them. When I heard my mum's voice today it was like there was so much of everything in it – pain, anger – and although she was arguing about me I knew there was a lot more to what she was saying than just me. I just don't understand adults. If she wasn't happy, why didn't she just leave? Well anyway, I'm glad I'm leaving for a while.'

'Me too,' said Zulma.

24

The morning we left, we all met at Mrs B's house. She had two gifts for me and Zulma – mine was a necklace made of tiny sea-shells threaded with a piece of string – some of the shells were broken, but when Mrs B held it up, each shell caught its own bit of sunlight and glowed; it was beautiful.

'Is that for me?' I asked.

'I was wearing it when I ran away, I always believed it brought me luck, good luck. My mammy made it for me. One year we went to the coast to some relations and I collected these shells; she got some string and made it for me. I've always kept it. Here you have it now, I'm not running anywhere any more, am I? Come, let me put it on for you.

'For Zulma,' she said, 'I made something to remind her of us . . .' It was a sampler, cross-stitched with two little girls, one black, the other brown, holding hands, and the words, 'Margaret, Zulma, Harriet,' below them. 'You can hang it in your room Zulma.'

'Thank you Mrs B, thank you,' said Zulma.

'Your mammies are waiting downstairs, but I want to say something to you both now. Come,' and she patted the bed where she was sitting. 'The good Lord saw fit not to give me any children, though God knows, we would have liked one at least. But I think he, or she – the jury is still out on that one – has more than made up for that for he's given me two beautiful daughters – both of you – I couldn't want for more, and I'm real honoured I could help you both and your mammies.

'Zulma, I know you worried about your mammy, but she'll

come through. Her agreeing to send you back is a good sign. I don't think she believed he would ever beat her the way he did, her mind is made up – at least for now – not to go back to him. Give her time – that's what she needs now, time. And she will be staying with me for a while – how's that?'

Zulma smiled; I knew she was really worried about her mother going back to her stepfather and him beating her again. This way at least she wouldn't have that to worry her.

Mrs B went on: 'Your mammy loves you, Zulma, she's just a little confused about her husband. She knows now there's no reason to confuse you too. So give her time, men come and men go, but a mother's love is always there, always. You don't know what she been through to bring you here in this world and here in Canada for that matter. Your gran loves you and wants you there, you want to be there, that's a whole lot more than a lot of folks have, right girls?

'And you Margaret – Harriet,' she chuckled. 'You know your mammy going to be o.k.' I nodded. 'Cuthbert may play good dominoes, and think he's God but he can act real foolish sometimes, which is how he's been acting over you. He's also a decent man, remember that. He'll have a whole heap of thinking and feeling to do over the summer but I sense that Tina is coming into her own. She'll be able to handle him, and he might become a better man out of all this.

'I know both of you sad to go, but grieving and crying are important, don't bottle it up. It's real and it means you still alive, don't forget that. Time to get worried is when you stop feeling pain. But enough preaching Bertha.' She laughed, pulled us close and made a sound, like she was laughing and crying. 'All right girls, time to go. I have some food for you – never know what crap they'll feed you on that plane. Nothing like good food to keep a perspective on things. Come on, come on, your mammies must be wondering what we doing so long up here.'

146

25

If anyone had told me I would be up in a plane, *with the help of my mother*, listening to Zulma go on about her dreams, I would have called them a liar – but there I was, up in this humungous jet, on the way to Tobago. Of all the uncool things to have happen to me on my first big trip away from my family – I go and fall asleep. I couldn't even keep myself awake for the movie. It must have been because I was up late the night before worrying about everything – my mother, Zulma's mother, if my father was going to be really, really mean to my mum – everything, I worried about everything. I even worried about the plane crashing and wondered if I should make a will and leave all my records to Ti-cush; and I almost went into Jo-Ann's room and asked her to look out for Mum, but I decided against it. I didn't think Jo-Ann would understand what was worrying me; she was too involved with herself and her problems. For so long I had envied her my parents' attention and understanding. Things had been so easy for her, almost too easy for her, but she would never understand Mum the way I now understood her . . . and suddenly I was sorry for Jo-Ann.

I had lots of dreams that night; I don't remember much about them, except for the one in which I am carrying old Mrs Blewchamp on my back, and running after Harriet Tubman. The old lady got heavier and heavier in the dream, then suddenly we were underground, in caves, and I could hear the slave-owners and dogs above us. Mrs Blewchamp smiled at me and brought her twisted fingers up to her lips and motioned for me to be silent, then she showed me the numbers on her wrist –

they glowed red in the dark cave. I reached out to touch the numbers and suddenly there I was in my bed wide awake, hearing my heart beating.

When I fell asleep again after worrying some more, I dreamt about Zulma's island. I don't remember exactly what it was I dreamt, but when I came awake I knew I had been dreaming about Tobago, and the following day, when I stopped being cool and fell asleep on the plane, my dreams picked up where those of the night before left off – I knew it although I could remember nothing of the night before.

I am sitting at a table shelling peas, pigeon peas, a huge mountain of pigeon peas. I try to climb this mountain but keep sliding back and back and laughing. To make the mountain smaller I begin to eat the peas – they taste raw and sweet – yuck! I spit them out, and now they form themselves into little families all different colours: some a soft pearl-white, others clear lime-smelling green, some a dark and shiny brown, others white and flecked with brown.

Zulma and I are falling, falling into the mountain of peas, with a bump we land on the seashore; waves come in with a roar, make a gurgling sound as they leave the beach and leave a trail of lace – sea lace. I pick it up, the lace, drape it over me and Zulma, around my waist, down my legs, until I am all sea lace. I dive deep into the sea, the sea lace swims away, and I come from the sea wearing a dress of shimmering blue and green. I pull some more sea lace and wrap it around my head and I sing, sing to the sea about the sea.

Zulma disappears – into a shell – a huge conch shell. I follow up into the shiny pink inside of the shell, the world is pink as I slide all around the smooth pink inside, pink like I have never seen before – of early dawns and sunsets, like Harriet Tubman would have watched – pink roses and satin ribbons, rabbits' noses; the rough pink of cats' tongues, and the smooth moist pink of babies' tongues, pink, pink like the pigeon-pea flowers, Zulma says, and the pale pink of chenettes, the pinkest of pinks – the palest yet deepest of pinks.

148

What was that? A soft yet definite roar, of the sea you always heard when you put the shell to your ear – but it was getting louder and louder – I had to get out, where was Zulma? Oh, the noise was so loud, I had to get out.

I opened my eyes and looked at Zulma; she was still asleep. I closed my eyes again, and there was Zulma, giant crabs were chasing her, with giant claws and eyes on stalks. 'You shouldn't have opened the pail, Zulma,' I said. 'Gran said not to.'

'Me know.' The crabs were gone, but there was Barbara, Zulma's goat; Zulma had helped Gran pull her out when she was born, and she followed Zulma around ever since – everywhere. She also ate everything that came her way – books, dresses, grass, table-cloths and now Zulma and I watched as she ate Gran's house. Gran was trying to pull her away – she had just eaten the kitchen; now she was going to eat Zulma's bed.

'Stop it,' I yelled, 'stop it.'

I opened my eyes; Zulma was looking at me laughing.

'Is what you dreaming about?'

'You and your goat.'

'Me too.' We both cracked up.

'It was going to eat your bed.'

Suddenly the pilot's voice, 'Ladies and gentlemen, to your left is the island of Barbados.'

'Do you hear that, Zulma? Barbados.' We peered through the window. 'Gee it's pretty – I didn't think it would be so pretty. Look at all those red roofs and the sea, it's so blue. It's nice isn't it? I wonder why he left?'

The image was gone so quickly, but not from my mind. I was thinking of the tiny, perfect island I had just seen. I wished the plane could have stood still over it for a while so I could look some more.

The pilot's voice again: 'Ladies and gentlemen, please fasten your seatbelts in preparation for landing at Piarco International Airport.'

We looked at each other and gripped each other's hands.

149

'I suppose this is it, eh?' I said.

'Dis is it, dis is it, and somewhere out dere is Gran.' The plane bumped once – Zulma gave a tiny scream – twice and it sped on. We had landed. Zulma was home – well almost home.

We had just finished customs, when Zulma pulled at me: 'Look Margaret, dere she is, look!'

I looked where Zulma was pointing and saw a tall thin woman, Zulma's gran. I was a little nervous – she did look a little fierce.

'Come on, Margaret, come on,' said Zulma. She was wearing the same blue ribbons she wore the day I first met her. These were bouncing up and down as she rushed towards her gran who walked towards us slowly; something seemed the matter with one of her legs – Gran limped. Zulma was running toward her and they were hugging each other – I could tell they had wanted to do this for a long time – too long.

'Gran, Gran, me miss you so much, so much.'

Gran didn't answer, or if she did, it was too low for me to hear, but I could see her face tighten – it looked like she was in pain – I could see the tears on her cheeks.

Zulma was home. I watched them and remembered the first day I met Zulma, the day we made angels in the snow. She had been unhappy then, now was happy – actually she was more than happy – it was like she held happiness inside her. And I was happy too.

'So dis is Margaret, hello Margaret.'

'Yes Gran, dis is me special friend. How you say it Margaret, ab-so-lute, friend? Is thanks to she, Gran, why me here today.'

'Don't forget your prayers, Zulma,' I said. We laughed.

Gran looked at me and smiled. She should smile more often I thought; it made her face much nicer.

'Thank you Margaret,' the voice was rough, almost harsh. 'Thank you for bringing Zulma back, she belong here. Come now, children, your uncle Herbert waiting – come on, let we go.'

150